Trade Policies and Developing Nations

Integrating National Economies: Promise and Pitfalls

Barry Bosworth (Brookings Institution) and Gur Ofer (Hebrew University)
Reforming Planned Economies in an Integrating World Economy

Ralph C. Bryant (Brookings Institution)
International Coordination of National Stabilization Policies

Susan M. Collins (Brookings Institution/Georgetown University)
Distributive Issues: A Constraint on Global Integration

Richard N. Cooper (Harvard University)
Environment and Resource Policies for the World Economy

Ronald G. Ehrenberg (Cornell University)
Labor Markets and Integrating National Economies

Barry Eichengreen (University of California, Berkeley)
International Monetary Arrangements for the 21st Century

Mitsuhiro Fukao (Bank of Japan)
Financial Integration, Corporate Governance, and the Performance of Multinational Companies

Stephan Haggard (University of California, San Diego)
Developing Nations and the Politics of Global Integration

Richard J. Herring (University of Pennsylvania) and Robert E. Litan (Department of Justice/Brookings Institution)
Financial Regulation in the Global Economy

Miles Kahler (University of California, San Diego)
International Institutions and the Political Economy of Integration

Anne O. Krueger (Stanford University)
Trade Policies and Developing Nations

Robert Z. Lawrence (Harvard University)
Regionalism, Multilateralism, and Deeper Integration

Sylvia Ostry (University of Toronto) and Richard R. Nelson (Columbia University)
Techno-Nationalism and Techno-Globalism: Conflict and Cooperation

Robert L. Paarlberg (Wellesley College/Harvard University)
Leadership Abroad Begins at Home: U.S. Foreign Economic Policy after the Cold War

Peter Rutland (Wesleyan University)
Russia, Eurasia, and the Global Economy

F. M. Scherer (Harvard University)
Competition Policies for an Integrated World Economy

Susan L. Shirk (University of California, San Diego)
How China Opened Its Door: The Political Success of the PRC's Foreign Trade and Investment Reforms

Alan O. Sykes (University of Chicago)
Product Standards for Internationally Integrated Goods Markets

Akihiko Tanaka (Institute of Oriental Culture, University of Tokyo)
The Politics of Deeper Integration: National Attitudes and Policies in Japan

Vito Tanzi (International Monetary Fund)
Taxation in an Integrating World

William Wallace (St. Antony's College, Oxford University)
Regional Integration: The West European Experience

Anne O. Krueger

Trade Policies and Developing Nations

THE BROOKINGS INSTITUTION
Washington, D.C.

Library of Congress Cataloging-in-Publication data:
Krueger, Anne O.
Trade policies and developing nations/
Anne O. Krueger
p. cm.—(Integrating national economies)
Includes bibliographical references and index.
ISBN 0-8157-5956-0 (cl. : alk. paper).—ISBN 0-8157-5055-2 (pbk. : alk. paper)
1. Developing countries—Commercial policy. 2. Developing
countries—Foreign economic relations. 3. Developing
countries—Commerce. 4. Import substitution—Developing countries.
I. Title. II. Series.
HF1413.K73 1995
382′.3′091724—dc20   94-5148
                                                                CIP

9 8 7 6 5 4 3 2 1

The paper used in this publication meets the minimum requirements of
American National Standard for Information Sciences—Permanence of Paper
for Printed Library Materials, ANSI Z39.48-1984

Typeset in Plantin

Composition by Princeton Editorial Associates
Princeton, New Jersey

Printed by R. R. Donnelley and Sons Co.
Harrisonburg, Virginia

Foreword

B EFORE THE 1980s most developing countries, following policies of "import substitution," tried to reduce their dependence on the international economy by protecting new domestic industries. They were bystanders rather than participants in the design of the international trading system under the General Agreement on Tariffs and Trade, seeking preferential treatment for their exports rather than taking part in multilateral trade negotiations.

By the 1980s it was clear that those import-substitution policies had failed, and most developing countries began opening up their economies and integrating them into the international economic system. They participated actively in the Uruguay Round of trade negotiations, obtaining changes from the developed countries on import restrictions on textiles and apparel, among other items. They made concessions on their own trade policies, especially on intellectual property rights and trade-related investment measures.

In this book Anne O. Krueger traces the reasons for the developing countries' reversals of earlier policies and demonstrates the importance of the open international trading system for them. The Uruguay Round agreement, the entrance of Spain and Portugal into the European Communities, and the rapid pace of economic reform in the developing countries illustrate their adaptability.

The author notes that developing nations in general should be willing to enter into arrangements for deeper integration. These measures, however, must promote the efficient working of the international economy. Two measures advocated for deeper integration—labor standards and environmental protection—are fraught with danger. Protectionists in the developed countries have seized on these issues, which could hinder the legitimate exports of the developing countries to developed ones, rather than increase international trading efficiency.

The author concludes that developing countries also need more time than developed nations to implement the steps needed for successful integration. They must complete the first phases of policy reform and market opening to be ready to integrate. As long as they receive the time they need, and the efficiency of the international trading system is given primary attention, developing nations should be able to continue their deeper integration.

The author wishes first and foremost to acknowledge her debt to the organizers of the Integrating National Economies project—Henry Aaron, Ralph Bryant, Susan Collins, and Robert Lawrence. Not only did they initiate the project and organize a valuable session for participants, they were invaluable commentators on the work in progress.

Rapid changes in the international trading arrangements that have been occurring as the manuscript was in progress made this book unusually difficult to complete. Not only was the North American Free Trade Agreement implemented but the Uruguay Round was completed with enormous implications for developing countries' trade policies and the possibilities of deeper integration. The author thanks all four organizers for their patience and thoughtful comments as the work was in progress.

She is indebted to all of the project participants for their helpful comments on an earlier draft of this manuscript. She thanks Benni Ndulu and Dani Rodrik for especially helpful comments and suggestions. She appreciates Roderick Duncan's able research assistance throughout the project.

At Brookings Theresa Walker edited the manuscript, and David Bearce verified it. Colette M. Solpietro, Anita G. Whitlock, and Paige Oeffinger provided word processing. Princeton Editorial Associates prepared the index.

Funding for the project came from the Center for Global Partnership of the Japan Foundation, the Curry Foundation, the Ford Foundation, the Korea Foundation, the Tokyo Club Foundation for Global Studies, the United States–Japan Foundation, and the Alex C. Walker Educational and Charitable Foundation. The author and Brookings are grateful for their support.

The views expressed here are those of the author and should not be ascribed to the people or organizations whose assistance is acknowledged above or to the trustees, officers, or staff members of the Brookings Institution.

BRUCE K. MACLAURY
President

May 1995
Washington, D.C.

Contents

Tables

Preface to the Studies on Integrating National Economies

*E*CONOMIC interdependence among nations has increased sharply in the past half century. For example, while the value of total production of industrial countries increased at a rate of about 9 percent a year on average between 1964 and 1992, the value of the exports of those nations grew at an average rate of 12 percent, and lending and borrowing across national borders through banks surged upward even more rapidly at 23 percent a year. This international economic interdependence has contributed to significantly improved standards of living for most countries. Continuing international economic integration holds out the promise of further benefits. Yet the increasing sensitivity of national economies to events and policies originating abroad creates dilemmas and pitfalls if national policies and international cooperation are poorly managed.

The Brookings Project on Integrating National Economies, of which this study is a component, focuses on the interplay between two fundamental facts about the world at the end of the twentieth century. First, the world will continue for the foreseeable future to be organized politically into nation-states with sovereign governments. Second, increasing economic integration among nations will continue to erode differences among national economies and undermine the autonomy of national governments. The project explores the opportunities and tensions arising from these two facts.

Scholars from a variety of disciplines have produced twenty-one studies for the first phase of the project. Each study examines the heightened competition between national political sovereignty and increased cross-border economic integration. This preface identifies background themes and issues common to all the studies and provides a brief overview of the project as a whole.[1]

Increasing World Economic Integration

Two underlying sets of causes have led nations to become more closely intertwined. First, technological, social, and cultural changes have sharply reduced the effective economic distances among nations. Second, many of the government policies that traditionally inhibited cross-border transactions have been relaxed or even dismantled.

The same improvements in transportation and communications technology that make it much easier and cheaper for companies in New York to ship goods to California, for residents of Strasbourg to visit relatives in Marseilles, and for investors in Hokkaido to buy and sell shares on the Tokyo Stock Exchange facilitate trade, migration, and capital movements spanning nations and continents. The sharply reduced costs of moving goods, money, people, and information underlie the profound economic truth that technology has made the world markedly smaller.

New communications technology has been especially significant for financial activity. Computers, switching devices, and telecommunications satellites have slashed the cost of transmitting information internationally, of confirming transactions, and of paying for transactions. In the 1950s, for example, foreign exchange could be bought and sold only during conventional business hours in the initiating party's time zone. Such transactions can now be carried out instantaneously twenty-four hours a day. Large banks pass the management of their worldwide foreign-exchange positions around the globe from one branch to another, staying continuously ahead of the setting sun.

Such technological innovations have increased the knowledge of potentially profitable international exchanges and of economic opportunities abroad. Those developments, in turn, have changed consumers' and producers' tastes. Foreign goods, foreign vacations, foreign financial investments—virtually anything from other nations—have lost some of their exotic character.

---

1. A complete list of authors and study titles is included at the beginning of this volume, facing the title page.

Although technological change permits increased contact among nations, it would not have produced such dramatic effects if it had been countermanded by government policies. Governments have traditionally taxed goods moving in international trade, directly restricted imports and subsidized exports, and tried to limit international capital movements. Those policies erected "separation fences" at the borders of nations. From the perspective of private sector agents, separation fences imposed extra costs on cross-border transactions. They reduced trade and, in some cases, eliminated it. During the 1930s governments used such policies with particular zeal, a practice now believed to have deepened and lengthened the Great Depression.

After World War II, most national governments began—sometimes unilaterally, more often collaboratively—to lower their separation fences, to make them more permeable, or sometimes even to tear down parts of them. The multilateral negotiations under the auspices of the General Agreement on Trade and Tariffs (GATT)—for example, the Kennedy Round in the 1960s, the Tokyo Round in the 1970s, and most recently the protracted negotiations of the Uruguay Round, formally signed only in April 1994—stand out as the most prominent examples of fence lowering for trade in goods. Though contentious and marked by many compromises, the GATT negotiations are responsible for sharp reductions in at-the-border restrictions on trade in goods and services. After the mid-1980s a large number of developing countries moved unilaterally to reduce border barriers and to pursue outwardly oriented policies.

The lowering of fences for financial transactions began later and was less dramatic. Nonetheless, by the 1990s government restrictions on capital flows, especially among the industrial countries, were much less important and widespread than at the end of World War II and in the 1950s.

By shrinking the economic distances among nations, changes in technology would have progressively integrated the world economy even in the absence of reductions in governments' separation fences. Reductions in separation fences would have enhanced interdependence even without the technological innovations. Together, these two sets of evolutionary changes have reinforced each other and strikingly transformed the world economy.

Changes in the Government of Nations

Simultaneously with the transformation of the global economy, major changes have occurred in the world's political structure. First, the number of governmental decisionmaking units in the world has expanded markedly, and political power has been diffused more broadly among them. Rising nationalism and, in some areas, heightened ethnic tensions have accompanied that increasing political pluralism.

The history of membership in international organizations documents the sharp growth in the number of independent states. For example, only 44 nations participated in the Bretton Woods conference of July 1944, which gave birth to the International Monetary Fund. But by the end of 1970, the IMF had 118 member nations. The number of members grew to 150 by the mid-1980s and to 178 by December 1993. Much of this growth reflects the collapse of colonial empires. Although many nations today are small and carry little individual weight in the global economy, their combined influence is considerable, and their interests cannot be ignored as easily as they were in the past.

A second political trend, less visible but equally important, has been the gradual loss of the political and economic hegemony of the United States. Immediately after World War II, the United States by itself accounted for more than one-third of world production. By the early 1990s the U.S. share had fallen to about one-fifth. Concurrently, the political and economic influence of the European colonial powers continued to wane, and the economic significance of nations outside Europe and North America, such as Japan, Korea, Indonesia, China, Brazil, and Mexico, increased. A world in which economic power and influence are widely diffused has displaced a world in which one or a few nations effectively dominated international decisionmaking.

Turmoil and the prospect of fundamental change in the formerly centrally planned economies compose a third factor causing radical changes in world politics. During the era of central planning, governments in those nations tried to limit external influences on their economies. Now leaders in the formerly planned economies are trying to adopt reforms modeled on Western capitalist principles. To the extent that these efforts succeed, those nations will increase their economic involvement with the rest of the world. Political and economic alignments among the Western industrialized nations will be forced to adapt.

Governments and scholars have begun to assess these three trends, but their far-reaching ramifications will not be clear for decades.

Dilemmas for National Policies

Cross-border economic integration and national political sovereignty have increasingly come into conflict, leading to a growing mismatch between the economic and political structures of the world. The effective domains of economic markets have come to coincide less and less with national governmental jurisdictions.

When the separation fences at nations' borders were high, governments and citizens could sharply distinguish "international" from "domestic" policies. International policies dealt with at-the-border barriers, such as tariffs and quotas, or responded to events occurring abroad. In contrast, domestic policies were concerned with everything behind the nation's borders, such as competition and antitrust rules, corporate governance, product standards, worker safety, regulation and supervision of financial institutions, environmental protection, tax codes, and the government's budget. Domestic policies were regarded as matters about which nations were sovereign, to be determined by the preferences of the nation's citizens and its political institutions, without regard for effects on other nations.

As separation fences have been lowered and technological innovations have shrunk economic distances, a multitude of formerly neglected differences among nations' domestic policies have become exposed to international scrutiny. National governments and international negotiations must thus increasingly deal with "deeper"—behind-the-border—integration. For example, if country A permits companies to emit air and water pollutants whereas country B does not, companies that use pollution-generating methods of production will find it cheaper to produce in country A. Companies in country B that compete internationally with companies in country A are likely to complain that foreign competitors enjoy unfair advantages and to press for international pollution standards.

Deeper integration requires analysis of the economic and the political aspects of virtually all nonborder policies and practices. Such issues have already figured prominently in negotiations over the evolution of the European Community, over the Uruguay Round of GATT negotiations, over the North American Free Trade Agreement (NAFTA), and over the bilateral economic relationships between Japan and the United States. Future debates about behind-the-border policies will occur with increasing frequency and prove at least as complex and contentious as the past negotiations regarding at-the-border restrictions.

Tensions about deeper integration arise from three broad sources: cross-border spillovers, diminished national autonomy, and challenges to political sovereignty.

Cross-Border Spillovers

Some activities in one nation produce consequences that spill across borders and affect other nations. Illustrations of these spillovers abound. Given the impact of modern technology of banking and securities markets in creating interconnected networks, lax rules in one nation erode the ability of all other nations to enforce banking and securities rules and to deal with fraudulent transactions. Given the rapid diffusion of knowledge, science and technology policies in one nation generate knowledge that other nations can use without full payment. Labor market policies become matters of concern to other nations because workers migrate in search of work; policies in one nation can trigger migration that floods or starves labor markets elsewhere. When one nation dumps pollutants into the air or water that other nations breathe or drink, the matter goes beyond the unitary concern of the polluting nation and becomes a matter for international negotiation. Indeed, the hydrocarbons that are emitted into the atmosphere when individual nations burn coal for generating electricity contribute to global warming and are thereby a matter of concern for the entire world.

The tensions associated with cross-border spillovers can be especially vexing when national policies generate outcomes alleged to be competitively inequitable, as in the example in which country A permits companies to emit pollutants and country B does not. Or consider a situation in which country C requires commodities, whether produced at home or abroad, to meet certain design standards, justified for safety reasons. Foreign competitors may find it too expensive to meet these standards. In that event, the standards in C act very much like tariffs or quotas, effectively narrowing or even eliminating foreign competition for domestic producers. Citing examples of this sort, producers or governments in individual nations often complain that business is not conducted on a "level playing field." Typically, the complaining nation proposes that *other* nations adjust their policies to moderate or remove the competitive inequities.

Arguments for creating a level playing field are troublesome at best. International trade occurs precisely because of differences among nations—in resource endowments, labor skills, and consumer tastes. Nations specialize in producing goods and services in which they are relatively most efficient. In a fundamental sense, cross-border trade is valuable because the playing field is *not* level.

When David Ricardo first developed the theory of comparative advantage, he focused on differences among nations owing to climate or technology. But Ricardo could as easily have ascribed the productive differences to differing "social climates" as to physical or technological climates. Taking all "climatic" differences as given, the theory of comparative advantage argues that free trade among nations will maximize global welfare.

Taken to its logical extreme, the notion of leveling the playing field implies that nations should become homogeneous in all major respects. But that recommendation is unrealistic and even pernicious. Suppose country A decides that it is too poor to afford the costs of a clean environment, and will thus permit the production of goods that pollute local air and water supplies. Or suppose it concludes that it cannot afford stringent protections for worker safety. Country A will then argue that it is inappropriate for other nations to impute to country A the value they themselves place on a clean environment and safety standards (just as it would be inappropriate to impute the A valuations to the environment of other nations). The core of the idea of political sovereignty is to permit national residents to order their lives and property in accord with their own preferences.

Which perspective about differences among nations in behind-the-border policies is more compelling? Is country A merely exercising its national preferences and appropriately exploiting its comparative advantage in goods that are dirty or dangerous to produce? Or does a legitimate international problem exist that justifies pressure from other nations urging country A to accept changes in its policies (thus curbing its national sovereignty)? When national governments negoti-ate resolutions to such questions—trying to agree whether individual nations are legitimately exercising sovereign choices or, alternatively, engaging in behavior that is unfair or damaging to other nations—the dialogue is invariably contentious because the resolutions depend on the typically complex circumstances of the international spillovers and on the relative weights accorded to the interests of particular individuals and particular nations.

Diminished National Autonomy

As cross-border economic integration increases, governments ex-perience greater difficulties in trying to control events within their borders. Those difficulties, summarized by the term *diminished auton-omy*, are the second set of reasons why tensions arise from the compe-tition between political sovereignty and economic integration.

For example, nations adjust monetary and fiscal policies to influ-ence domestic inflation and employment. In setting these policies, smaller countries have always been somewhat constrained by foreign economic events and policies. Today, however, all nations are con-strained, often severely. More than in the past, therefore, nations may be better able to achieve their economic goals if they work together collaboratively in adjusting their macroeconomic policies.

Diminished autonomy and cross-border spillovers can sometimes be allowed to persist without explicit international cooperation to deal with them. States in the United States adopt their own tax systems and set policies for assistance to poor single people without any formal cooperation or limitation. Market pressures operate to force a degree of de facto cooperation. If one state taxes corporations too heavily, it knows business will move elsewhere. (Those familiar with older debates about "fiscal federalism" within the United States and other nations will recognize the similarity between those issues and the emerging international debates about deeper integration of national economies.) Analogously, differences among nations in reg-ulations, standards, policies, institutions, and even social and cultural preferences create economic incentives for a kind of arbitrage that erodes or eliminates the differences. Such pressures involve not only the conventional arbitrage that exploits price differentials (buying at one point in geographic space or time and selling at another) but also shifts in the location of production facilities and in the residence of factors of production.

In many other cases, however, cross-border spillovers, arbitrage pressures, and diminished effectiveness of national policies can produce unwanted consequences. In cases involving what economists call externalities (external economies and diseconomies), national governments may need to cooperate to promote mutual interests. For example, population growth, continued urbanization, and the more intensive exploitation of natural resources generate external diseconomies not only within but across national boundaries. External economies generated when benefits spill across national jurisdictions probably also increase in importance (for instance, the gains from basic research and from control of communicable diseases).

None of these situations is new, but technological change and the reduction of tariffs and quotas heighten their importance. When one nation produces goods (such as scientific research) or "bads" (such as pollution) that significantly affect other nations, individual governments acting sequentially and noncooperatively cannot deal effectively with the resulting issues. In the absence of explicit cooperation and political leadership, too few collective goods and too many collective bads will be supplied.

Challenges to Political Sovereignty

The pressures from cross-border economic integration sometimes even lead individuals or governments to challenge the core assumptions of national political sovereignty. Such challenges are a third source of tensions about deeper integration.

The existing world system of nation-states assumes that a nation's residents are free to follow their own values and to select their own political arrangements without interference from others. Similarly, property rights are allocated by nation. (The so-called global commons, such as outer space and the deep seabed, are the sole exceptions.) A nation is assumed to have the sovereign right to exploit its property in accordance with its own preferences and policies. Political sovereignty is thus analogous to the concept of consumer sovereignty (the presumption that the individual consumer best knows his or her own interests and should exercise them freely).

In times of war, some nations have had sovereignty wrested from them by force. In earlier eras, a handful of individuals or groups have questioned the premises of political sovereignty. With the profound increases in economic integration in recent decades, however, a larger number of individuals and groups—and occasionally even their national governments—have identified circumstances in which, it is claimed, some universal or international set of values should take precedence over the preferences or policies of particular nations.

Some groups seize on human-rights issues, for example, or what they deem to be egregiously inappropriate political arrangements in other nations. An especially prominent case occurred when citizens in many nations labeled the former apartheid policies of South Africa an affront to universal values and emphasized that the South African government was not legitimately representing the interests of a majority of South Africa's residents. Such views caused many national governments to apply economic sanctions against South Africa. Examples of value conflicts are not restricted to human rights, however. Groups focusing on environmental issues characterize tropical rain forests as the lungs of the world and the genetic repository for numerous species of plants and animals that are the heritage of all mankind. Such views lead Europeans, North Americans, or Japanese to challenge the timber-cutting policies of Brazilians and Indonesians. A recent controversy over tuna fishing with long drift nets that kill porpoises is yet another example. Environmentalists in the United States whose sensibilities were offended by the drowning of porpoises required U.S. boats at some additional expense to amend their fishing practices. The U.S. fishermen, complaining about imported tuna caught with less regard for porpoises, persuaded the U.S. government to ban such tuna imports (both direct imports from the countries in which the tuna is caught and indirect imports shipped via third countries). Mexico and Venezuela were the main countries affected by this ban; a GATT dispute panel sided with Mexico against the United States in the controversy, which further upset the U.S. environmental community.

A common feature of all such examples is the existence, real or alleged, of "psychological externalities" or "political failures." Those holding such views reject untrammeled political sovereignty for nation-states in deference to universal or non-national values. They wish to constrain the exercise of individual nations' sovereignties through international negotiations or, if necessary, by even stronger intervention.

The Management of International Convergence

In areas in which arbitrage pressures and cross-border spillovers are weak and psychological or political externalities are largely absent, national governments may encounter few problems with deeper integration. Diversity across nations may persist quite easily. But at the other extreme, arbitrage and spillovers in some areas may be so strong that they threaten to erode national diversity completely. Or psychological and political sensitivities may be asserted too powerfully to be ignored. Governments will then be confronted with serious tensions, and national policies and behaviors may eventually converge to common, worldwide patterns (for example, subject to internationally agreed norms or minimum standards). Eventual convergence across nations, if it occurs, could happen in a harmful way (national policies and practices being driven to a least common denominator with externalities ignored, in effect a "race to the bottom") or it could occur with mutually beneficial results ("survival of the fittest and the best").

Each study in this series addresses basic questions about the management of international convergence: if, when, and how national governments should intervene to try to influence the consequences of arbitrage pressures, cross-border spillovers, diminished autonomy, and the assertion of psychological or political externalities. A wide variety of responses is conceivable. We identify six, which should be regarded not as distinct categories but as ranges along a continuum.

National autonomy defines a situation at one end of the continuum in which national governments make decentralized decisions with little or no consultation and no explicit cooperation. This response represents political sovereignty at its strongest, undiluted by any international management of convergence.

Mutual recognition, like national autonomy, presumes decentralized decisions by national governments and relies on market competition to guide the process of international convergence. Mutual recognition, however, entails exchanges of information and consultations among governments to constrain the formation of national regulations and policies. As understood in discussions of economic integration within the European Community, moreover, mutual recognition entails an explicit acceptance by each member nation of the regulations, standards, and certification procedures of other members. For example, mutual recognition allows wine or liquor produced in any European Union country to be sold in all twelve member countries even if production standards in member countries differ. Doctors licensed in France are permitted to practice in Germany, and vice versa, even if licensing procedures in the two countries differ.

Governments may agree on rules that restrict their freedom to set policy or that promote gradual convergence in the structure of policy. As international consultations and monitoring of compliance with such rules become more important, this situation can be described as *monitored decentralization*. The Group of Seven finance ministers meetings, supplemented by the IMF's surveillance over exchange rate and macroeconomic policies, illustrate this approach to management.

Coordination goes further than mutual recognition and monitored decentralization in acknowledging convergence pressures. It is also more ambitious in promoting intergovernmental cooperation to deal with them. Coordination involves jointly designed mutual adjustments of national policies. In clear-cut cases of coordination, bargaining occurs and governments agree to behave differently from the ways they would have behaved without the agreement. Examples include the World Health Organization's procedures for controlling communicable diseases and the 1987 Montreal Protocol (to a 1985 framework convention) for the protection of stratospheric ozone by reducing emissions of chlorofluorocarbons.

Explicit harmonization, which requires still higher levels of intergovernmental cooperation, may require agreement on regional standards or world standards. Explicit harmonization typically entails still greater departures from decentralization in decisionmaking and still further strengthening of international institutions. The 1988 agreement among major central banks to set minimum standards for the required capital positions of commercial banks (reached through the Committee on Banking Regulations and Supervisory Practices at the Bank for International Settlements) is an example of partially harmonized regulations.

At the opposite end of the spectrum from national autonomy lies *federalist mutual governance*, which implies continuous bargaining and joint, centralized decisionmaking. To make federalist mutual governance work would require greatly strengthened supranational institutions. This end of the management spectrum, now relevant only as an analytical benchmark, is a possible outcome that can be imagined for the middle or late decades of the twenty-first century, possibly even sooner for regional groupings like the European Union.

Overview of the Brookings Project

Despite their growing importance, the issues of deeper economic integration and its competition with national political sovereignty were largely neglected in the 1980s. In 1992 the Brookings Institution initiated its project on Integrating National Economies to direct attention to these important questions.

In studying this topic, Brookings sought and received the co-operation of some of the world's leading economists, political scientists, foreign-policy specialists, and government officials, representing all regions of the world. Although some functional areas require a special focus on European, Japanese, and North American perspectives, at all junctures the goal was to include, in addition, the perspectives of developing nations and the formerly centrally planned economies.

The first phase of the project commissioned the twenty-one scholarly studies listed at the beginning of the book. One or two lead discussants, typically residents of parts of the world other than the area where the author resides, were asked to comment on each study.

Authors enjoyed substantial freedom to design their individual studies, taking due account of the overall themes and goals of the project. The guidelines for the studies requested that at least some of the analysis be carried out with a non-normative perspective. In effect, authors were asked to develop a "baseline" of what might happen in the absence of changed policies or further international cooperation. For their normative analyses, authors were asked to start with an agnostic posture that did not prejudge the net benefits or costs resulting from integration. The project organizers themselves had no presumption about whether national diversity is better or worse than international convergence or about what the individual studies should conclude regarding the desirability of increased integration. On the contrary, each author was asked to address the trade-offs in his or her issue area between diversity and convergence and to locate the area, currently and prospectively, on the spectrum of international management possibilities running between national autonomy through mutual recognition to coordination and explicit harmonization.

HENRY J. AARON   SUSAN M. COLLINS
RALPH C. BRYANT   ROBERT Z. LAWRENCE

Chapter 1

Growth Prospects, Trade, and Access to Markets

*F*OR THE past half century the developing countries have grappled with their relationship to the world trading system, the role of their trade policies in their economic growth, and the influence of the world economy on their prospects for growth. These issues have been contentious and emotional. As evidence from the experience of the developing countries has mounted and the world economy has evolved, the focal points of contention have shifted.

Introduction

In the 1950s and 1960s, while the industrialized countries were removing their trade barriers and lowering their tariffs to increase the openness of their economies, most developing countries were pursuing policies of "import substitution," thus insulating their economies from the rest of the world. By the 1980s, however, policymakers in most developing countries had concluded that import-substitution policies had exhausted their usefulness or had never been useful. They were therefore opening their economies to trade.

Even as that happened, however, the global economy and international economic system were changing. With the costs of transport and communications falling, and the trade liberalization that took place, producers in industrialized countries were becoming sensitive even to small changes in the international economy. Calls for "harmonization" of standards, "fair trade," and further integration of many economic policies increased. Proposals that would

1

result in common standards, in increasing uniformity of competition policy, or in alignment of other domestic economic policies are calls for deeper integration.

Some of those calls are expressions of legitimate concern about the efficiency of the global economy; others are little more than disguised calls for insulation from pressures of global competition.

But regardless of motivation, several items have been placed on the international agenda for consideration. In some cases, the proponents of change have in mind primarily their concerns about competitors in other developed countries. Until the 1980s, it would have been—largely correctly—assumed that developing countries would automatically remain outside any such arrangements for deeper integration.

However, many developing countries are integrating with the world economy, and proposals for deeper integration should take into account their likely effects on developing countries. For, as will be seen, the growth prospects of the developing countries hinge crucially on the growth of a healthy international trading system and their access to it. If industrialized countries agree on deeper integration measures that compel developing countries to incur very high costs or lose their access to international markets, the consequences for the prospects for growth of developing countries could be serious.[1] At the same time, some developing countries have already become sufficiently important traders that their inclusion in the system is important to the developed countries. Means must be found—as measures of deeper integration are adopted—of inducing those developing countries to participate without their suffering unacceptably high costs.

This book analyzes the probable impact of various proposals for deeper integration. To do so requires first an understanding of the evolution of the developing countries' relationship with the global economy and the lessons that have been learned from experience to date. In light of those lessons, the key measures that the industrialized countries might take for deeper integration and their potential effect on the developing countries can be evaluated.

In this chapter I analyze the interaction of developing countries and the world economy from the late 1940s to the early 1990s, concluding with a survey of the situation as of the mid-1990s and a

---

1. There are also questions, in some instances, about the feasibility for some developing countries of undertaking some proposed measures of deeper integration. See chapter 3.

review of the lessons on which most analysts would agree. Chapter 2 examines the role of the developing countries in GATT and the international trading system. Chapter 3 provides an analysis of the opportunities and dangers for developing countries that could arise were some of the frequently voiced proposals for deeper integration enacted. Policy implications of the analysis are also explored.

The Importance of Trade and Markets

The international economy is important to all countries, most especially the developing ones. Those developing countries that have grown rapidly for several decades have by and large adopted outer-oriented growth strategies, under which the fast growth of exports has been a notable characteristic. They have high fractions of gross domestic product (GDP) originating in exports and are closely integrated with the world economy. Those countries whose growth has accelerated more recently have generally been successful in part by changing incentives so that their integration with the world economy would increase. Prospects for their sustained growth depend significantly on continued rapid expansion of trade. For countries that have been less successful in achieving rapid growth, primary commodity exports still provide the financing for imports of capital and intermediate goods that are vital for their economies.

But although the importance of trade to developing countries has long since been recognized, policies and understanding of that relationship have changed profoundly. Most of that change has occurred in the past decade and a half and resulted in efforts to change trade policies, made with varying speed and differing conviction.

Early Mistakes under Import Substitution

The field of economic development was a new one after World War II. As countries were embarking on deliberate development programs to raise living standards and reduce poverty, there was limited experience with governmental responsibility for these activities. Since that time, knowledge has progressed enormously: the ideas that drove initial policy decisions led to some unanticipated results, which led to the rethinking of some of the ideas that had initially predominated.

Simultaneously, the contrasting experience of developing countries under differing policy regimes has enabled economists to bring evidence to bear to increase understanding of the development process. Among the essential insights that have emerged is that international trade and the international economy are instrumental in affecting the developing countries' growth prospects and their ability to improve the living standards of the poor. These insights are most readily understood in historical context.

There are three key aspects of this experience: the initial economic circumstances and economic policies undertaken to raise living standards and accelerate development; the experience of the East Asian countries; and the debt crisis and its lessons.

INITIAL CIRCUMSTANCES AND POLICIES. In the years after World War II, many developing countries attained their independence from their former colonial rulers. Although some countries, including most of Latin America, had earlier been independent, a strong sense prevailed in all of the developing countries that they had been economically dependent on the richer countries, and that their low living standards were directly related to that dependence. In all the developing countries, newly independent or otherwise, raising living standards through rapid economic growth became a primary political objective: colonialism and "economic imperialism" were blamed for low living standards.

Developing countries also had a strong sense of solidarity. Not only was it thought that the colonial, or at least economic, ties to the richer countries formed a common historical heritage, but developing countries also experienced a great similarity in economic circumstances. Indeed, for most intents and purposes, one could at that time say that most developing countries had characteristics in stark contrast to those of developed countries. Compared with the high per capita incomes in industrialized countries, poverty in the developing countries resulted from and led to a number of other similarities among them in virtually all dimensions.

The attributes of peoples' economic and social circumstances in most developing countries were very similar compared with those in developed countries, again largely as a result of the common factor—low standards of living. Most of the population—often 70 or more percent—were rural, and much of agricultural production was for subsistence and outside the market economy. Agricultural productivity was very low, with agricultural output nonetheless accounting for close to half of GDP in most countries.[2]

The prevalence of poverty resulted in other similar attributes. Malnutrition was commonplace. Life expectancies were very short, with high rates of infant (and maternal) mortality, and high death rates because of endemic diseases such as malaria as well as malnutrition. Life expectancy for women in India in the early 1950s, for example, was estimated to be less than thirty years. The educational attainments of the populations of almost all developing countries, with high rates of illiteracy and few persons with advanced technical or other education, were very low contrasted with developed countries. Even today, in many developing countries less than half the population has received enough formal schooling to be classified as literate.

Although poverty caused these abject results, it also led to a vicious circle: there were few teachers, doctors, hospital facilities, or other facilities with which to improve educational attainments and health conditions because incomes were low. Incomes were low partly because of the dearth of educational opportunities and lack of access to health and other services.

But just as health and educational facilities were in scarce supply, so, too, was other infrastructure. Roads were few and poorly maintained; railroad networks and capacity were small (but then, so, too was the volume of traffic to be carried); telephones, electricity generated, and passenger miles of traffic per person were all small fractions of their provision in developed countries. More important, there were very few factories, and a very small set of manufacturing activities, compared with that in developed countries. To the casual observer this difference in the relative importance of manufacturing seemed highly significant. Indeed, in the early years, many observers focused on the low availability of "physical capital" per person as the chief contributor to under-

2. To be sure, on close inspection, there were significant differences among developing countries. Some started with much more infrastructure and "human capital" than others (Sri Lanka, for example, had a population whose educational attainments were much greater than those of people in most developing countries); some (such as much of Africa, Thailand, and Brazil) apparently had open frontiers with little pressure of population while others, such as India and Korea, had little scope for extensive cultivation. There were even significant differences in per capita income levels, with Latin American countries generally much more affluent than South and East Asian ones. All of these differences, however, were dwarfed by the sharp contrast between developing and developed countries.

development. It was even thought that simply raising savings rates, and therefore investment rates, to increase capital per person would be the key to development.[3]

In the 1950s all developing countries were predominantly highly specialized in the production of primary commodities for export, and they imported most of their manufactured products. The little local manufacturing that existed was largely confined to light consumer ' goods such as textiles, matches, and edible oils.[4] This state of affairs led to "dependence" on foreign exchange earnings for imports of many important consumer goods, such as pharmaceuticals, and also for many capital goods. Most policymakers in developing countries saw this specialization of production in primary commodities as an outcome of colonial rule, and modernization was seen as synonymous with increasing the domestic productive capabilities for nontraditional commodities.[5]

Along with the similarities in observable economic characteristics, attitudes toward economic policy were much the same in most developing countries.[6] There was a general distrust of markets and a belief that governments could more effectively organize and lead economic activity, with regulation and control of such private economic activity

3. See Krueger and others (1989, chap. 2), for a fuller exposition of prevalent thinking about development in the early postwar period.

4. This perception, like many others, was not entirely accurate. India, for example, had had an iron and steel industry that was competitive by world standards since the early 1900s. And many Latin American countries had experienced rapid growth of their manufacturing sectors in the 1920s and 1930s. Nonetheless, the variety of manufactured products produced in all developing countries was certainly much smaller than that in developed countries, and the fraction of export earnings that originated from exports of primary commodities was very high. Thus, if taken as a statement of fact, the proposition that developing countries had little manufacturing capability was false. If taken as a statement relative to developed countries, however, it had considerable truth to it.

5. That domestic productive capacity for nontraditional items would increase with growth was a correct prediction. However, as has subsequently been learned, growth itself results from increasing productivity of labor (through provision of more and better capital per worker, through more education and training, and through introduction and adoption of improved techniques) and the increased diversification that accompanies growth is primarily a result, rather than a cause, of growth.

6. Reasons for these similarities included the legacy of the Great Depression with its impact on the developing countries; the then-widespread belief that the Soviet Union represented a "success" story of development; the spread of ideas among developing countries, especially under the intellectual leadership of people such as Jawaharlal Nehru of India and Raul Prebisch of Argentina; and the worldwide spread of "development economics" as a separate field within economics in which the normal paradigms were said not to apply.

as there was.[7] A widespread suspicion of the international economy also prevailed, with many observers holding that the reliance of developing countries on primary commodities had contributed to, if not caused, their continued poverty.[8] Some analysts, reversing the Malthusian forecasts, insisted that the terms of trade would inevitably turn against primary commodities. Perhaps even more important, on the basis of the association of differences in per capita income with different proportions of economic activity in agriculture, most members of the "modernizing elite" in virtually every developing country believed that development would necessarily imply industrialization. Furthermore, it was thought that new industries would not be able to compete with the ones already established in developed countries.

Hence, it was planned to encourage rapid industrial development through raising the rate of capital formation and allocating a large share of the new capital stock to investment in import-substitution industries, and in the infrastructure—electricity, transport, and communications—that would be needed to support it. The idea behind import substitution was that rapid industrialization would take place as imports would be replaced by expansion of output of (protected) domestically produced goods as domestic capacity was created.

Indeed, in the 1950s it was widely believed that developing countries should protect their domestic industries both on infant industry grounds and because it was thought that export earnings from primary commodities would not grow rapidly enough to meet the increasing demand for machinery, equipment, and other imports thought essential for raising investment levels and levels of industrial activity.

The infant industry argument, known since the days of List and Alexander Hamilton, stated the case for support of a new industry

7. From the perspective of the 1990s, this view seems naive. However, at the time it was shared by most economists. The legacy of the 1930s had shattered the belief that the market was self-correcting, and leaders in developing countries also believed that private markets had been used to improve living standards in developed countries and to suppress them in developing countries. As late as 1984, however, even such a respected economist as Tinbergen was able to assert that the nature of ownership of enterprises was immaterial, and that what mattered was the quality of management.

8. Indeed, it was widely held that the colonial powers had achieved their higher standards of living by seeing to it that manufacturing was their prerogative and that developing countries should specialize in the manufacture of raw materials, then sold cheaply to the colonial powers.

under certain circumstances. One, the new industry would initially be high cost, but it would experience such cost reductions after its start-up that it would eventually become sufficiently competitive on world markets to repay the start-up costs with an adequate return on the "investment" in its initial losses. Two, the industry would not be privately profitable to start up because some of the initial expenditures would lead to productivity increases (externalities) that would not be captured by those undertaking the initial investment.[9]

As if the infant industry argument were not enough to rationalize import substitution, pessimism about elasticity was also widespread. Here, the view was that the income elasticity of demand for primary commodities was relatively low and the price elasticity of demand even lower. Hence, it was thought that export expansion would result in price decreases so that prospects for growth of foreign exchange earnings, given the existing structure of exports, were poor relative to the rate at which the demand for foreign exchange could be expected to grow in the absence of import substitution.

ESTABLISHMENT AND RESTRICTIVENESS OF TRADE REGIMES.   As a consequence, in many developing countries, foreign trade regimes were established, not for the primary purpose of maintaining a comfortable balance-of-payments position, but rather to support the industrialization-import substitution push. Initially, provision was made for high levels of protection once domestic productive capacity was established in a certain line of activity. In many countries, imports of particular goods were licensed, and ultimately prohibited, as domestic production capacity was deemed sufficient to supply the domestic market.[10] At the same time, efforts were made to encourage imports of capital goods and of intermediate goods and raw materials used in "import-substituting" industries. The primary means for achieving this aim was to keep protection rates for inputs and capital goods low.

With those incentives, domestic producers began establishing and expanding capacity in import-competing industries. Initially, growth

9. Even then, it was widely recognized that a production subsidy could achieve the same results in terms of inducements to an infant industry as could a tariff without imposing such large costs on consumers (including user industries). Advocates of infant industry protection, however, believed that most governments were sufficiently short of revenues that a tariff was the only feasible means of providing infant industry protection. For critiques of the infant industry argument, see Baldwin (1969); Krueger (1990a).

10. See Bhagwati and Srinivasan (1974) for a description of the trade regime in India; and Krueger (1975) for Turkey.

of industrial output was fairly rapid. In several industries import substitution was fairly easy, in the sense that the newly established industries used relatively unskilled labor-intensive processes to produce goods for which a sizable domestic market existed. These opportunities were among the first to be exploited by domestic entrepreneurs, as the profitability of investment behind a wall of protection was assured.

Rapid growth of industrial output also meant that the demand for imported capital goods to equip the factories, intermediate goods, and raw materials also rose rapidly. Although import substitution was taking place, it was import intensive in demands for capital equipment and intermediate goods, and export growth was inadequate to generate supplies of foreign exchange equal to the rapidly rising demand.[11]

However, partly because little attention was paid to export growth, and partly because focus on import-competing industries and strong incentives for investment in import-substitution industries were diverting resources away from export industries, export earnings failed to grow as rapidly as real output. Certainly these earnings increased less rapidly than did the demand for foreign exchange to support the import-substituting industrialization. Most developing countries quickly experienced "foreign exchange shortages." As that happened, the foreign trade and payments regime was altered in order to "conserve scarce foreign exchange" for those purposes believed most directly associated with economic growth.

The major means of conservation was the licensing of imports. Goods deemed less essential for developmental purposes were at first restricted, and then, as foreign exchange shortages intensified, banned. As foreign exchange difficulties intensified over time, import licenses even for goods associated with development projects were restricted.

During the 1950s and 1960s, policymakers throughout the world were very reluctant to change the nominal value of their currencies. This opposition was perhaps even more true of leaders in newly

11. As first pointed out by Carlos Diaz-Alejandro (1965), import-substitution policies were "import-intensive." Not only did investment in new or additional capacity generally have a very high import component for the machinery and equipment, but usually import-substitution factories were designed in anticipation of a large proportion of imported intermediate goods and raw materials. The result was that import-substitution was not "foreign exchange saving."

independent countries, where nationalist pride was associated with exchange rates. However, it was also thought that raising the price of foreign exchange would make investment goods—thought to be the primary determinant of the rate of economic growth—more expensive. The response to balance of payments "shortages," therefore, was often to restrict imports through licensing and other quantitative mechanisms even more strongly than encouragement of import substitution would have warranted.

In many developing countries, including those in Latin America, the Middle East and North Africa, South Asia, and Africa, therefore, trade regimes became more and more restrictive and "inner-oriented." Incentives for producing a dollar's worth of international value added in import-competing industries were five, ten, and even more times the incentives for producing a dollar's worth of international value added in export industries. Indeed, producers of import-competing goods had little incentive to expand capacity of existing lines of production more rapidly than domestic demand grew. They could instead invest in a new line of activity, with prospects of a sheltered, usually monopolistic, position in the domestic market. When confronted with a choice between competition on the international market at international prices, and a sheltered domestic market at much higher domestic prices, there was a strong pull of resources in favor of the latter as the safer and more profitable alternative.

Simultaneously, most developing countries were experiencing rates of inflation above those in most industrialized countries. In large part, these higher inflation rates were the result of large and growing fiscal deficits, as expenditures on development programs (for infrastructure, increased health and educational services, and investment in public sector manufacturing enterprises started within the government sector) grew at rates in excess of the rate at which governmental revenues, including foreign aid, could be increased. At fixed nominal exchange rates, which authorities reluctantly changed too little, too late, incentives for exports were decreased further.

Little wonder that exports, of manufactures and of primary commodities, grew slowly, if at all, in most countries pursuing import-substitution policies.[12] With the rapid growth in demand for imports,

12. Indeed, developing countries' shares of the world market in agricultural commodities and minerals also fell as investment continued to be directed away from these "tradi-

and the sluggish growth in foreign exchange earnings, the restrictiveness of trade regimes increased rapidly. By the mid-1960s, it was widely believed that an almost-universal characteristic of developing countries was a chronic shortage of foreign exchange.

STOP-GO CYCLES. Despite their efforts to maintain the nominal exchange rate fixed, most developing countries' governments eventually confronted a situation in which import licensing had been so restricted that something had to be done.[13] Usually, this response was triggered when a "foreign exchange crisis" occurred. By that time, the situation was usually extreme, as exporters were withholding goods from the market in the anticipation of a more favorable export price at a later date, and importers were stockpiling because imports were expected to become more expensive. Often, industrial production was sharply curtailed because of shortages of raw materials, intermediate goods, or spare parts. Capital flight in anticipation of a possible devaluation intensified the problems.

Although in some countries the deterioration in the economic situation was permitted to proceed much further than in other countries, pressures in most cases finally became strong enough to provoke changes. Sometimes, changes were cosmetic and half-hearted, and the crisis quickly returned. In most cases, however, efforts were made to modify the system. Usually, it was necessary for the authorities to approach the International Monetary Fund (IMF) (and other official sources of funds) for support in "stabilizing" the economy.

The usual pattern was that the International Monetary Fund would then lead a consortium in support of policy change in the country in question. These changes would normally include "austerity" measures to reduce the demand for foreign exchange, a change in the nominal exchange rate, some liberalization of the trade regime, and several other reforms. These programs were called "stabilization" programs.[14]

---

tional" export activities. Developing countries' share of exports of agricultural commodities fell from 44 percent in 1955 to 28 percent in 1980. By 1990, developing countries' shares were once again increasing. See table 2-1 in this volume. See Krueger (1990b) for details.

13. There was usually an intermediate stage when exchange rates were altered for some transactions, but not others, giving rise to chaotic de facto multiple exchange rate regimes. Often, the resulting unwieldiness of the regime was an important motivating factor in exchange rate changes. The particulars, however, are not important for present purposes. See Bhagwati (1978) for an account.

14. See the essays in Cline and Weintraub (1981); and in Williamson (1983) for details.

Stabilization programs generally included a change in the nominal exchange rate; a reduction in the prospective size of the fiscal deficit; increases in nominal interest rates (which were often so low that real interest rates were negative); and some liberalization and rationalization of the trade regime.[15]

A stop-go pattern developed in country after country. A development plan led to significant planned increases in investment and real income. As that plan was implemented, the demand for imports generally grew more rapidly than had been anticipated, while foreign exchange earnings grew more slowly. Import licensing was adjusted to become more restrictive, but the resulting shortages and delays acted as a brake on economic growth. As demand continued to outstrip supply, the costs of foreign exchange shortage mounted. Finally, a crisis was reached and a reform program undertaken.

These crises took different forms and were of varying severity. In many instances, short-term credits, mostly suppliers' credits, had been used to finance imports and foreign exchange had been unavailable to repay them. When foreigners were no longer to provide even suppliers' credits to finance imports, even imports of essential items could dry up quickly. One dramatic case was in Turkey in 1958, where the unavailability of imported petroleum meant that there was no means of transporting harvested crops to port until reforms were started.

For most of the developing countries, a foreign exchange shortage (or crisis induced by rapidly rising inflation) culminated in a stabilization program, which usually resulted in a slowdown in economic activity. That reduced the demand for imports and increased the supply of exports, and the foreign exchange "shortage" eased.[16] With

15. Several measures were specific to particular countries' circumstances in policies. In Turkey, for example, the authorities attempted to control inflation by preventing increases in the prices of goods produced by State Economic Enterprises from 1956 to 1958. But these enterprises' costs were rising at about the rate of inflation, with the result that they were incurring ever-larger deficits. These deficits were normally covered by Central Bank credits and thus fueled the very inflation that the price controls were designed to avoid. In Turkey, therefore, increasing the prices of goods produced by public sector enterprises was normally part of the "stabilization package." Krueger (1975, pp. 44–45).

16. Besides a slowdown in domestic economic activity, several other factors contributed to that result. First, there were often IMF and World Bank resources supporting the program. Those resources immediately increased foreign exchange availability and permitted a flow of imports. Second, the long delays that usually took place before the need for stabilization programs (and especially devaluation) was recognized usually had led to large

that easing, government policies began reverting to their status quo ante: development plans anticipated increased levels of investment along with imports, and the cycle was repeated. Although policies had been temporarily altered to cope with foreign exchange difficulties, there was no intent to change the fundamental thrust of policy, and once again the growth of demand for foreign exchange outstripped the growth of supply, as the cycle repeated itself.

Most policymakers and development economists initially blamed the vagaries of the international market for these stop-go cycles. Two-gap models of economic growth were developed, in which there were two constraints to growth: the availability of savings and the availability of foreign exchange.[17] In these models, the growth rate of exports was exogenously given by world demand conditions, while demand for foreign exchange grew more rapidly the higher the rate of investment and the rate of growth of income. Hence, when the growth of demand for foreign exchange outstripped the growth of supply, it could happen that there was inadequate foreign exchange to permit new investments even to the level permitted by domestic savings. In the atmosphere of "export pessimism" of the 1950s and 1960s, it was not thought that exports from developing countries could grow more rapidly if their own economic policies were altered.

It was not until the 1980s that experience was to demonstrate that the problems confronting developing countries were fundamentally more deep-seated than that of stop-go cycles and that foreign exchange shortage was more a symptom than a cause of the problems.

Most developing countries experienced this broad pattern, although the particulars varied depending on the fortunes of each country's export commodities and its development policies. Vagaries of the international market, weather variations affecting crop and export magnitudes from year to year, and other factors obscured an important underlying phenomenon: as the stop-go cycles repeated,

---

speculative capital outflows; when the stabilization program was undertaken, these were normally reversed. For the same reasons, exporters had often delayed exporting in anticipation of currency devaluation, increasing export earnings once it had taken place while importers had attempted to build up stocks prior to devaluation and then started selling from inventory once a program was announced. Third, the exchange rate change and related policy shifts also induced an increased supply of, and reduced domestic demand for, import-competing and export goods.

17. The best exposition of the two-gap model is that in Chenery and Strout (1966).

successive go periods became somewhat shorter and entailed lower rates of growth than had earlier cycles. The stop parts of the cycle, by contrast, were longer and often entailed a greater slowdown in economic activity.

Besides these cycles of restrictiveness of the trade regime and growth, over time there was a secular trend, initially largely obscured by the magnitude of the cycles: trade regimes in many countries in Latin America, the Middle East, North Africa, Sub-Saharan Africa, and Asia were becoming more restrictive and inner oriented, and growth was slowing. Each "go" period of the cycle was somewhat shorter, and growth was at a lower rate unless terms-of-trade changes were highly favorable. Each "stop" was more painful than the preceding one. And, while savings and investment rates were rising, the result was an increasing capital-output rate and *not* more satisfactory growth. Along with these phenomena, the restrictiveness of trade and payments regimes was increasing from cycle to cycle, and inefficiencies associated with those regimes were increasing. In Turkey, for example, a first "stop" was in 1958; growth rates had fallen to about 2 percent in the two preceding years. In 1970 a second "stop" took place in a buoyant world environment, though the average growth rate had been slower. A third "stop," in 1980, had been preceded by two years of falling real GDP and a much lower average growth rate over the decade. In 1980 the Turkish government made major policy changes in response.

Until the 1980s, however, this deceleration in growth rates was not widely recognized. A few countries, however, adopted different economic policies prior to the 1980s, and their experience illuminates some of the problems inherent in import-substitution industrialization strategies.

Experience of East Asian NICs

Stabilization programs in developing countries were intended to meet the immediate problem of "foreign exchange crisis." These crises were not regarded as symptomatic of longer-term difficulties, but rather of short-term macroeconomic imbalances or possibly adverse changes in the international economy. Hence, little or no consideration was given to making fundamental changes in economic policies. In the 1950s and 1960s in most countries, once foreign exchange accumulated after the onset of a stabilization program, the basic policy stance toward industrialization through import substitution remained unaltered, policies were once again oriented to accelerating economic growth, and the "go" phase of the cycle resumed.

The exception was in East Asia. The experience in that region diverged sharply from that of most other countries. Hong Kong, Korea, Singapore, and Taiwan—collectively called the East Asian NICs (newly industrializing countries)—all adopted very similar policies, and all experienced remarkable acceleration in growth rates and improvements in all aspects of economic performance.[18] It took the debt crisis of the 1980s for analysts to appreciate more fully the lessons of the East Asian experience, understanding of which is central to the development prospects of other developing countries.

INITIAL SITUATION. Korea and Taiwan followed import-substitution policies, similar to those just described, in the 1950s. Each encountered severe economic difficulties, in Taiwan because of the disruption resulting from immigration and perceived defense needs and in Korea because of the dislocations resulting from the Korean War.

In both cases, per capita incomes were extremely low. Korea was estimated to have one of the lowest per capita incomes among Asian countries. Indeed, in the 1950s the economic problems confronting Taiwan and Korea were, if anything, more pronounced than those facing most developing countries.

Economic policy was chaotic as foreign exchange shortages and domestic inflation intensified. In both cases, there were multiple exchange rates, highly restrictive import licensing regimes, sluggish growth of foreign exchange earnings, large gaps between foreign exchange earnings and receipts covered mostly by inflows of foreign aid, and rapid inflation fueled in part by large fiscal deficits. As in other developing countries, what exports there were were almost

18. Focus here is on the Korean and Taiwanese experience for two reasons. First, those economies were substantially larger than the Hong Kong and Singaporean economies, and many observers tended to discount the experience of the latter two because of their city-state status. Second, in broad outline the experience of the four was sufficiently alike that examination of each of their experiences is unnecessary. Singapore was part of Malaya until the mid-1960s and had much the same experience in that Singapore had earlier been part of a Malayan import-substitution regime. It adopted outer-oriented trade policies as part of the growth strategy after the mid-1960s. Hong Kong was different only in that the British government of the crown colony had never adopted protectionist policies; Hong Kong is regarded as a close approximation to a laissez-faire policy regime.

entirely primary commodities, and savings rates were extremely low. Indeed, in the 1950s in Korea, exports averaged less than 4 percent of GDP, of which almost 90 percent were primary commodities. Foreign aid, equal to about 10 percent of GDP, enabled imports equal to about 13 percent of GDP and covered almost all of investment as domestic savings were negligible.

FUNDAMENTAL POLICY REFORMS.   However, Taiwan in the mid-1950s and Korea in the early 1960s responded to their foreign exchange crises and rising inflation rates with policy changes much more far reaching than those undertaken in other countries with stabilization programs. For various reasons, they decided to shift development strategies and to attempt to grow by relying on comparative advantage and by using the international economy in that effort.[19]

Initial policy reforms in Taiwan and Korea included the measures normally part of stabilization programs but also contained steps designed to assure producers that successful exporters would garner strong and stable rewards. At first, these incentives were provided through various add-ons to the exchange rate as an offset to the existing high protection for production of import-competing goods. Over time, however, these add-ons diminished in importance, protection for import-competing producers was reduced, and the exchange rate was maintained at realistic levels and adjusted frequently to compensate for differentials in inflation rates.

This commitment to encouraging the development of exports—known as an outer-oriented trade strategy—was achieved in various ways. On one hand, the add-ons to the exchange rate offset the protection accorded to import-competing producers, thus reducing the "bias" of the trade regime toward import substitution. Although incentives were not provided primarily through the exchange rate, the reward to exporters was fairly uniform per dollar of exports, without regard to the nature of the commodity manufactured.[20] On the other

19. The U.S. authorities made clear to the Koreans that foreign aid would be reduced starting in the late 1950s. Because Korea relied on imports for a variety of primary commodities (including oil), Korean policymakers appear to have concluded that the only prospect for growth was through growth of exports. See Krueger (1979) for an account.

20. In the absence of policy intervention, one would expect that domestic relative prices of tradable goods were the same as their foreign prices. Economists refer to these relative prices as neutral. With protection for import-competing goods, domestic relative prices of import-competing goods are above their international levels, and the trade regime is said to

hand, protection for import-competing producers fell, because those wanting to encourage exports were impelled to permit producers of exportables to import needed items without severe restrictions. The freedom from restriction was essential to enable exporters to compete on an even footing with producers in other countries.

Besides reforms of the trade and payments regime and a sharp change in the earlier orientation toward import substitution, policymakers in all four East Asian NICs undertook other measures to increase the efficiency with which the economy functioned.[21] These included, among others, measures to reduce the distortionary impact of taxes, fiscal reforms to reduce fiscal deficits, and raising nominal interest rates above the rate of inflation, enabling exporters to purchase inputs at international prices without delays.

For present purposes, only one of these acts requires attention. That is, in all of the East Asian NICs, labor markets were deregulated so that few distortions were present. In contrast to many other countries, minimum wage legislation was abandoned, and few taxes were placed on employment of labor. Consequently, employment, especially in export-oriented activities, could rise rapidly. Once the unemployment rate (about 25 percent in Korea at the start of reforms) had fallen, increasing demand for labor resulted in rapid increases in real wages.

The Korean labor market was flexible, and Korean employers found it worthwhile to hire inexperienced workers. This situation was clearly important and will be discussed later in reference to calls for imposing labor standards upon developing countries. Most analysts of the East Asian experience agree that flexibility in the labor market was a necessary condition for the success of the outer-oriented trade strategy.[22]

Policymakers in each of the NICs address structural bottlenecks to the smoother functioning of their economies to this day. However, to

---

be "biased" in favor of import substitution because the reward for producing import-competing goods is greater than it would be in a neutral regime. Naturally, a regime that is biased in favor of import substitution is biased against production of exportables. If policymakers were to take measures that provided subsidies for exports, which were greater than the level of protection for import-competing goods, the regime would be said to be biased in favor of exportables. A regime cannot be biased in favor of both exportables and import-competing goods.

21. For accounts of the overall policy reform programs, on Korea see Frank, Kim, and Westphal (1975) and Mason and others (1980); on Taiwan, see Kuo (1983).

22. See, for example, World Bank (1993b).

understand how the international economy affects growth prospects for developing countries one must focus on the critical reforms and their effects in the trade and payments regimes.[23]

In a prevailing policy of import substitution, automatic protection implied sharply different rates of protection to different activities, depending on the level and price elasticity of domestic demand and the degree (usually small) of domestic competition. In contrast, incentives for exporting were offered on a uniform basis for virtually all economic activities. That is, in Korea all exporters received the same number of Korean won per dollar of foreign exchange earned. Import-competing producers in earlier years, however, received widely differing numbers of won per dollar depending on their line of activity. The same was true in Taiwan. Thus, whereas in import-substitution regimes producers of apparel might be afforded a protection rate of, say, 50 percent, while assemblers of radios might be operating behind a rate of several hundred percent, in Korea and Taiwan incentives to producers were related to dollars of exports earned without much regard for the type of item produced.

Furthermore, the evidence suggests that the export incentives provided by the trade and payments regime, besides being virtually uniform across economic activities, did not "bias" the regime greatly in favor of production for exporting as contrasted with production for import substitution.

Because the rate of incentive was almost uniform across activities and paid for out of government monies, several factors tended to restrain how much export incentives could exceed those provided by the exchange rate. The most important was that, as the authorities attempted to maintain "real" incentives for exporting by adjusting incentives as domestic inflation exceeded world rates, pressures for a change in the exchange rate and reductions in export incentives intensified. Consequently, a tendency occurred to reduce reliance on

23. No doubt the change in the trade and payments regime was critical in permitting rapidly accelerating growth rates in the East Asian NICs. There is a greater debate within academic circles about the extent to which exports were market driven or government led. Although that debate continues (see Rodrik [1993] for a recent summary), there is general agreement on the importance of trade reforms, the uniformity of incentives for exports, and the proposition that as growth continued, the possibility that government intervention might "guide" economic activity in ways that resulted in greater economic efficiency diminished.

Table 1-1. *Indicators of Korean Trade and Economic Performance,
1958–70*

Indicator	1958	1960	1963	1966	1968	1970
Real GDP (1960 = 100)	95.2	100.0	118.0	153.5	181.0	224.1
Exports (millions of U.S dollars)	17	31	87	250	486	882
Exports as percent of GDP	1.5	2.8	4.8	10.3	12.6	14.2
Imports (millions of U.S. dollars)	344	306	497	680	1322	1804
Imports as percent of GDP	10.7	12.7	15.9	21.2	25.2	25.6

Source: Author's calculations based on data from International Monetary Fund (1983, pp. 320–23).

tax credits, interest subsidies, and other measures fairly rapidly under
the outer-oriented trade regimes in comparison to the long periods
when high rates of protection conferred through restrictive import
licensing or import prohibitions went virtually unnoted.

GROWTH AFTER POLICY REFORMS. The results of the policy changes in
Korea and Taiwan are almost as astonishing in retrospect as they were at
the time. These countries started their reform with very low levels of
exports (and imports, which were constrained by import licensing procedures and the shortage of foreign exchange) even in relation to low
levels of per capita income, low savings rates, high inflation, and the
numerous other policy problems that plagued the economies of the
countries that had adopted import-substitution strategies.

The experience of Korea and Taiwan was similar enough so that
recounting the experience of one country—Korea—will suffice. Table 1-
1 gives data on some salient aspects of the Korean experience.

Korea's exports increased from a mere $31 million in 1960 to $882
million in 1970—a decade in which dollar prices of internationally
traded goods were virtually constant. This change reflected an average
annual growth of export earnings of more than 40 percent. Imports
also rose rapidly, from $306 million in 1960 to $1,804 million in 1970.
Part of this increase reflected the increase in exports, as exporters
were entitled to import duty-free needed raw materials, intermediate
goods, and anything else used in the production of exports, clearing
customs paperwork when they reexported.[24] But part of the increase
reflected liberalization of the import regime.

24. In fact, the automatic procedure for imports included a wastage allowance so that
exporters were permitted to import somewhat more than the amounts consumed in produc-

The changing structure of the Korean economy after the trade and exchange rate policy reforms is most clearly reflected in the rows giving exports and imports as a percentage of GDP.[25] As can be seen, exports were only 2.8 percent of GDP, and imports 12.7 percent in 1960; by 1970 the percentages were 14.2 and 25.6.[26] Thus, a structural change was taking place in Korea as both exports and imports were growing rapidly. In fact, the trade deficit remained almost a constant 10 percentage points of GDP, although financing changed during the decade from reliance on foreign aid to reliance on private commercial lending from international banks.

Although the dramatic and sustained increase in exports was the most striking characteristic of the Korean economy during the 1960s, the first row of table 1-1 shows the rapid increase in real GDP that accompanied it. Real GDP had grown only about 5 percent in the 1958–60 period, barely enough to maintain per capita income, given population growth. But it more than doubled in the subsequent decade, for an average annual growth in excess of 8 percent.

Exports of many goods and services grew rapidly, but a key feature was that growth of exports of labor-intensive industrial exports was spectacular in the initial years of the new growth strategy. Initially, this spurt was of course partly a consequence of the very small base from which export growth had started. But sustained growth continued. During the 1960s and early 1970s, most of the rapidly growing exports consisted of industrial products that used relatively large amounts of unskilled labor (compared with highly skilled workers such as technicians and engineers) and relatively little capital.[27]

This rapid growth of labor-using economic activities permitted a rapid increase in industrial employment. After the initial years, when unemployment fell dramatically, export industries were able to attract

ing exports. For present purposes, however, the more important point to note is that the Korean authorities immediately removed all obstacles to the duty-free importation of goods used by exporters, even before they were otherwise able to liberalize the import regime.

25. These numbers are influenced by changes in the real exchange rate. Between 1958 and 1960, for example, Korean imports fell in dollar terms. However, the change in the real exchange rate resulted in imports being an *increased* percentage of GDP, even though GDP grew during the period.

26. By 1990, exports of goods and services were 35.0 percent of GDP, while imports were 35.6 percent. Data from IMF (1993, p. 326).

27. See Frank, Kim, and Westphal (1975); and Hong (1981) for estimates of the factor inputs into Korean tradable goods.

additional employees only by raising their wages. Real wages almost doubled between 1960 and 1971 and then increased fourfold between 1971 and 1991.[28] Thus, throughout the period of rapid export growth after the mid-1960s, real wages were rising at annual rates of around 8 percent.

Over time, these changes resulted in a "structural transformation" of the entire economy. The percentage of the population and labor force in agriculture fell dramatically, reaching numbers not dissimilar to those in the developed countries by the 1990s. The percentage of exports *and* imports in GDP had, as seen in table 1-1, risen from 12 percent in 1958 to almost 40 percent in 1970 in Korea (and even higher shares in the other Asian NICs). Exports, which had been largely primary commodities in the 1950s, consisted almost entirely of industrial goods and services.

Moreover, the structure of exports was changing. As real wages rose and the labor forces acquired experience and training, producing the unskilled-labor-intensive goods that had been so profitable in the early years of the outer-oriented trade strategies became less attractive. Producers and exporters were entering into new activities in which the availability of skilled and highly trained labor had become a major asset (and more capital was available as a consequence of very high savings rates and of capital inflows). By the late 1980s and 1990s, production and exports of textiles and apparel, footwear, and other labor-intensive commodities that had earlier led in export growth were flagging, and producers were investing in offshore production facilities in South and Southeast Asia.

The use of foreign capital was also important. In the 1950s, as already noted, foreign aid financed virtually all of Korean investment. As growth accelerated, domestic savings rose, but so, too, did the profitability of investment. Foreign aid, however, was not increasing. The Korean policymakers therefore decided to rely on the private foreign capital market. During the 1960s, lending from private commercial banks to Korean firms financed much of the large gap between exports and imports seen in table 1-1. In some years, private foreign capital inflows were equal to around 10 percent of GDP. Given the high real rates of return on investment that could be realized, Korean debt rose rapidly, although the ratio of debt to GDP

---

28. See table 3-2 in this volume; and Krueger (1987, p. 197).

and debt to exports did not. Korea thus remained creditworthy and was able to gain access to the international capital market to permit a growth rate well above what would have been feasible if domestic savings had been the only source of financing for investment.

Private capital would probably not have flowed to Korea, and the flow certainly would not have been sustained, in the absence of the outer-oriented trade strategy. It was rapid export growth that enabled Koreans to continue borrowing over such a long interval. Until the late 1970s, almost all of the capital inflow consisted of borrowing from private commercial banks. By the late 1970s, however, direct foreign investment began flowing to Korea, and it, too, became a significant source of capital in the early 1980s, although domestic savings were rising and capital inflows as a percentage of GDP were falling by then. By the 1980s, Korean savings had grown sufficiently so that several years of sizable current account surpluses occurred, and a significant part of the debt was repaid.

Data for Taiwan tell a similar story. Export growth was extremely rapid, and estimates show that Taiwanese real per capita income grew slightly more rapidly than that of Korea. Taiwan relied somewhat more heavily on equity and direct foreign investment than did Korea, and less heavily on borrowing from abroad, and reached a position where domestic savings financed domestic investment earlier than did Korea.[29] By the 1980s, the four East Asian NICs, which had been among the poorest Asian countries in the 1950s, had the highest per capita incomes in Asia except for Japan. Although there were differences among the four NICs, all had grown through an outer-oriented, or export-oriented industrialization set of policies, under which incentives had been provided for exports, and export had grown rapidly.

It is not the purpose here to delve into the fine points of Korean, or other East Asian, policy changes. Suffice it to note three things. First, Korea and the other three NICs maintained their rates of growth of exports and of real GDP throughout the subsequent decades. Korean exports were $75 billion in 1992 and represented 32 percent of GDP in that year (up from 3 percent and $31 million in 1960). Imports were $77 billion, equal to about 33 percent of GDP. Thus, there was a structural change as both exports and imports grew. Second, the

29. By 1991 Taiwan held larger reserves of foreign exchange than any other nation in the world.

Table 1-2. *Growth of East Asian and Other Developing Countries,*
1960–87
Percent

Region	Real GDP growth		Total factor productivity growth	
	1960–73	*1973–87*	*1960–73*	*1973–87*
Developing countries				
Africa	4.0	2.6	0.7	−0.7
East Asia	7.5	6.5	2.6	1.3
Europe, Middle East, North Africa	5.8	4.2	2.2	0.6
Latin America	5.1	2.3	1.3	−1.1
South Asia	3.8	5.0	0.0	1.2
Developed countries				
Germany	4.3	1.8	1.9	0.9
United States	3.7	2.2	1.0	−0.1

Source: World Bank (1991, p. 43).

other three East Asian economies experienced similarly spectacular
and successful growth rates and increases in living standards, again
with exports a leading "engine of growth." Third, the sharp upward
shift in the real growth rate was accompanied by an initial drop in
unemployment and then rapid increases in urban employment, real
wages (an average of 8 percent annually), and living standards. Interestingly, the Korean and Taiwanese income distributions were among
the most equal in developing countries during this period of very
rapid growth.

LINKAGES BETWEEN OUTER-ORIENTED TRADE POLICIES AND GROWTH.
The dramatic differences that can be achieved with appropriate policies[30] and an outward trade orientation are widely recognized, although, as already mentioned, the precise mechanisms of causation
and the combination of supporting policies conducive to rapid economic growth are still subject to analysis. For the period from 1960 to
the late 1980s, the contrast in growth rates is evident in the data in
table 1-2. The first two columns give rates of growth of real GDP:
when it is recognized that some regions, such as Africa and South

30. It is widely recognized that an outer-oriented trade strategy cannot succeed unless
development of infrastructure (ports, roads, railroads, electric power, communications),
increasing educational attainments, and a number of other policies are conducive to growth.
See World Bank (1991) for a statement.

Asia, have higher rates of population growth (and therefore even lower rates of growth of per capita income) than others (such as East Asia and Latin America), the contrasts are even greater.

Although some in the 1970s attempted to argue that East Asia was "different," more recent successful policy reforms concerning the trade regime in countries such as Chile and Turkey in the 1980s have demonstrated that openness can yield greatly improved economic performance in other countries and even in adverse global environments.

What is important for later purposes is to attempt to understand the relationship between changes in trade policy and performance, on the one hand, and in the growth trajectory of the economy, on the other. Here, attention focuses on the advantages of an outer-oriented trade strategy for accelerating growth.

As already noted, outer-oriented trade strategies, as practiced by the East Asian NICs (and other latecomers in Southeast Asia and elsewhere more recently), are in fact policies that initially encourage exports at least enough to offset the "bias" of the trade regime toward import substitution. Over time, these strategies place greater and greater reliance on the exchange rate itself to provide incentives for resource allocation.

Initial steps in the process of transforming economic policies are always difficult, especially when policies used to carry out import substitution provide such a wide range of incentives for different industries. In part because some of the policies providing these incentives are difficult to remove, and in part because dramatic shifts are essential if policymakers are to convince private decisionmakers[31] that the reforms are genuine and that exporting really will be profitable, the early stages of policy reform normally entail the provision of incentives for export beyond those provided by the exchange rate.

The use of export subsidies in the early stages of the policy reform process in Korea has caused observers to question whether the reforms resulted in a free trade regime, or whether incentives were biased even more in favor of exports than under free trade.

Most estimates of the bias of the Korean trade and payments regime suggest that in the early stages of reform, the export incentives

---

31. In some instances, bureaucrats have been skeptical about the likely success of policy reform and have resisted implementing those actions desired by policymakers: politicians often need to make their reforms credible even to the public sector.

were really offsets to disincentives for exporting, and that the bias of the regime was very close to neutral (which is what a free trade stance would entail).[32]

Thus, there is considerable reason to interpret the Korean and other East Asian experience with export-led growth as arising out of the use of the international economy to enable the country to rely on comparative advantage in allocating resources. In an important sense, the initial success with export-led growth resulted from the country's ability to use its relative abundance of unskilled labor to produce goods and services that were relatively intensive in those factors and that required relatively less of physical and human capital. In the early stages of growth these resources were very scarce in Korea and Taiwan and remain scarce in countries such as India and Pakistan, which are only now beginning to change their highly protectionist trade regimes in an effort to achieve better economic performance and living standards.

In assessing the impact of deeper integration on developing countries, therefore, an important criterion is the extent to which they are enabled to rely on the international economy to achieve more satisfactory economic performance once policy reform is undertaken. As will be seen, many countries began the process of adjustment in the late 1980s and early 1990s. Measures of deeper integration that greatly delay or significantly reduce the benefits of opening their economies obviously impair growth prospects and may indeed make the political difficulties of shifting policies insurmountable.

The Turbulent 1970s

By the early 1970s, there was already a large observable difference between the development performance of the East Asian NICs and that of those developing countries that were still following policies based on government intervention and import substitution (see table1-2). Among these other countries, however, significant differences in growth performance also occurred. Some, such as Brazil and Turkey, had sustained rates of growth of real GDP in excess of 6 percent during the 1960s. Others, such as India, had done less well, with growth averaging less than 4 percent.[33] A few,

---

32. See the estimates in Frank, Kim, and Westphal (1975).

33. Because most developing countries were experiencing population growth rates in excess of 2 percent, the difference between 6–7 percent real growth and 4 percent real

including Indonesia prior to 1966, had failed to achieve any sustained increase in real per capita incomes.

Thus growth rates seemed to span a considerable range, and it was possible to believe that the East Asian NICs had had a very good decade, but that their growth was likely to slow.[34] Moreover, it did not seem that government controls and import-substitution policies were in any sense failing. Observers could point to countries with these policies that were experiencing very respectable track records. Indeed, as David Morawetz noted in assessing the first twenty-five years of development for the World Bank, the average rate of growth of real per capita incomes and living standards had been above that which had been forecast in the early days of development.[35]

There were indeed many successes for most developing countries in the 1950s and 1960s: death rates fell and life expectancies rose markedly; population growth appeared to be slowing even more than optimists had anticipated; educational attainments increased—dramatically in some cases; and, for most countries, efforts to provide agricultural research and extension services, irrigation, and other supports to rural areas had resulted in increased agricultural productivity at rates in excess of population growth.[36]

To be sure, growth rates were uneven, and not all countries were achieving similar success. With hindsight, identifying symptoms of underlying difficulties is straightforward. But the decade of the 1970s was turbulent for the world economy, and symptoms of decelerating growth were readily associated with the short-term fluctuations in the global economy, the consequent impact on countries' terms of trade, and other factors.

---

growth was a virtual doubling of the rate of growth of per capita income. Brazil and Turkey realized around 4 percent average annual growth of per capita income, in contrast with a rate of less than 2 percent for India.

34. Observers at the time tended to emphasize "special factors" in all four cases. Large quantities of U.S. foreign aid were often noted for Korea and Taiwan, even though aid was tapering off rapidly during the period when growth accelerated. Proximity to Japan was also noted, although Japan's share of Korean trade fell from over 50 percent to about 33 percent in the early 1960s. Indeed, Japan and Korea did not even sign a treaty ending hostilities after World War II until 1965.

In similar vein, the city-state status of Hong Kong and Singapore was noted as the circumstance that made their experience special.

35. Morawetz (1978).

36. One dramatic success came about because of the efforts to develop higher-yielding grains. The Green Revolution was a significant factor in these increases in agricultural productivity. For an account, see Evenson (1978).

It will be recalled that the oil price increase of 1973–74 constituted a major shock for most oil-importing developing countries. For many (both outer-oriented NICs and countries pursuing inner-oriented trade policies), the fourfold increase in the price of oil constituted a deterioration in the terms of trade equal to several percentage points of GDP. It resulted in a sudden sharp increase in the cost of imports with little or no increase in export earnings.

For oil-importing developing countries, adjustment to the oil price increase required measures to encourage additional exports, discourage imports, and reduce domestic expenditures relative to income over the longer term. In the shorter term, it was simply not feasible to increase export earnings or reduce imports rapidly enough to maintain earlier levels of the current account balance. Increased capital inflows could buy valuable time during which this adjustment could take place, and by doing so reduce the pain of adjustment, but they could not obviate the necessity for policy changes to adapt to the altered environment.

Hence, additional financing was required during a period when adjustment would take place.[37] Although some financing originated from oil exporters, bilateral aid agencies, and the multilateral institutions, many developing countries were able to finance a sizable share of their increased current account deficit by borrowing from private commercial banks in the developed countries.

The commercial banks were highly liquid with deposits from the oil exporters. They had found the East Asian NICs creditworthy and hence, when would-be borrowers appeared from other parts of the world, the bankers were happy to oblige. Thus the increased current account deficits of the developing countries were financed by a greatly increased flow of private capital in the form of commercial bank lending.

In a few developing countries, increased borrowing from commercial banks was accompanied by the necessary adjustment policies designed to restore the current account balance to a level sustainable given the prospective rate of capital inflows (policies included an increase in incentives for exporting, usually through devaluation).

---

37. The same was true of the oil-importing developed countries. However, for the most part those countries attempted to adjust by taking measures to restore current account balances to their pre-existing sizes.

In many countries, however, development strategies and economic policies continued unaltered, as increased borrowing from abroad permitted domestic expenditures, public and private, to keep growing despite the oil price increase. In the short run, this growth caused no apparent difficulties for two reasons.[38] First, given the availability of private capital from foreign commercial banks, growth rates of many of the developing countries did not fall. Indeed, on average they were above rates in developed countries in the latter part of the 1970s. Second, and equally important, many of the richer countries had responded to the worldwide recession of 1974 by expanding aggregate demand. In the context of a supply-shock-induced recession, these policies resulted predominantly in an acceleration of inflation with little increase in employment and output.

However, the resulting inflation of the latter half of the 1970s resulted in rapidly rising prices of the primary commodities that remained the major exports of most developing countries. In consequence, the dollar value of export earnings was rising rapidly, and hence the ratio of export earnings to debt-servicing obligations or debt was increasing slowly, if at all, for most developing countries, usually from an initial situation in which debt had been very small relative to GDP. The normal symptom of debtors' difficulties—that is, a high and rising debt-service ratio—was thus obscured.

To be sure, several countries encountered severe difficulties and approached the IMF for support in a stabilization program in the years after 1973. At the time, however, these crises and Fund-supported stabilization programs seemed related to the circumstances of the individual countries and not attributable to any systemic problem.

Turkey provided important instructive lessons for policymakers throughout the developing world in the 1980s. Turkey had undertaken Fund-supported stabilization programs in 1958 and 1970. In response to the 1970 devaluation and adjustment program foreign exchange earnings were still rising at the time of the first oil price

38. Indeed, at the time, many macroeconomists credited the developing countries' behavior with preventing the worldwide recession from having been more severe than it was. This was certainly true in the sense that the developing countries did maintain their expenditures on imports of commodities other than oil, which meant that demand dropped less dramatically for industrial countries' export industries than would otherwise have been the case.

increase, although domestic inflation was accelerating at a fixed nominal exchange rate. Turkey has virtually no domestic oil, and all petroleum products were imported by a state-owned enterprise.

After the 1973 oil price increase, no policy changes were made, so Turkish producers and consumers continued paying the same domestic price for oil as they had even though the world price had quadrupled. Turkey's current account swung sharply into deficit, and inflation, already running at about 25 percent annually, accelerated. Still, the government failed to respond, maintaining the nominal exchange rate despite the accelerating domestic inflation and worsening current account situation.

By 1976 Turkish growth was slowing down markedly, and Turkey was borrowing and increasing its foreign indebtedness rapidly. It did not take long, however, before lenders became reluctant to extend further credits. In the late 1970s, Turkish real GDP fell, as two efforts at IMF programs were abandoned, imports were curtailed because of the lack of availability of financing, and official export earnings declined sharply.

Finally, by 1980, inflation reached around 100 percent, while imports had dropped off so drastically that heating was unavailable for many people during the cold Anatolian winter.[39] At that point, after much internal debate, Turkish authorities responded to the crisis by announcing another program.[40] However, unlike earlier programs, it was stated from the beginning that the program would fundamentally alter the economy by making it more outer oriented, dismantling the restrictive import regime, relying much more heavily on the private sector for growth, and decontrolling much of the economy.

After the 1980 program started, growth resumed gradually at first and then more rapidly. Two of the results were highly significant. First, Turkish exports began growing rapidly and continued to do so throughout the decade, averaging around 20 percent annual growth (including the period of the worldwide recession in the early 1980s).

39. Although domestically produced coal and lignite were the major heating materials, deliveries had slowed because of the shortage of gasoline, which, of course, disrupted most economic activities.

40. A consensus seems to have developed among many groups that the old policies had basically failed, and that a new strategy for development would have to be undertaken. Thus, in contrast to the situation in many other countries, the Turks undertook their policy reforms when it was difficult to blame the international economy for their difficulties. See Krueger and Turan (1993) for an account of the Turkish reforms of the 1980s.

Consequently, the entire structure of the Turkish economy was transformed. Whereas exports and imports had averaged only 5 percent to 7 percent of GDP during the late 1970s, they each constituted around 20 percent of GDP by 1988. Second, any analysis of the problems confronting the Turkish economy in 1980 had to start with the recognition that Turkish domestic economic policies had been largely responsible for Turkey's economic difficulties. Even if one attempted to "blame" the 1973 oil price increase for subsequent problems, that accounted for a small percentage of the inflationary pressure, budgetary deficits, and other difficulties of the latter part of the 1970s.[41]

The Onset of the Debt Crisis

Turkey's experience was to be one of the very instructive episodes that informed the rethinking of development policies in the mid-1980s. The prelude to that rethinking was the "debt crisis," which began with the Mexican announcement in the summer of 1982 that Mexico could no longer voluntarily service its debts without additional foreign assistance. But by the time that announcement had occurred, many developing countries had been borrowing heavily and had increased their indebtedness greatly in 1980–82 because of the worldwide recession and associated events.

The worldwide inflation of the late 1970s had culminated in the second oil price increase of 1979. In contrast to the response after the first oil price increase, however, most industrialized countries, recognizing the limitations of expansionary policies in the face of supply-side shocks, responded by tightening monetary policy to avoid inflation.

The ensuing recession was far more severe and more prolonged than had been the recession of 1974–75. The prices of most commodities, which had been rising at rates at least equal to the rate of inflation, fell sharply in nominal terms, while the indebtedness of the borrowing developing countries increased sharply in response to the increased price of oil imports as well as the drop in the price of many of their export commodities. Moreover, lending by private banks, which had earlier charged fixed nominal interest rates, had gradually shifted to variable rates by the late 1970s. In consequence, when nominal interest rates rose sharply in the early 1980s interest obliga-

41. For a more detailed analysis, see Krueger and Aktan (1992, chap. 2).

tions on outstanding debt rose even more rapidly than outstanding debt increased (the price of most developing countries' exports were falling).

Thus debt of the developing countries rose from $141 billion in 1974 to $313 billion in 1978, an increase in the debt-service ratio from 11.8 to a still very manageable 18.4 percent.[42] But with export earnings falling rapidly and interest payments rising, countries had to borrow to finance their current account deficits when they could not reduce imports as rapidly as export earnings fell. Consequently, debt increased rapidly after that, rising to $430 billion in 1980, $546 billion in 1982 and $620 billion in 1983. That increase occurred from an initial position in 1979 with a much higher debt-service ratio: by 1982, the aggregate for all developing countries had reached more than 20 percent. Even that number obscured large differences between countries.[43]

Mexico was an oil exporter. The discoveries of oil fields in the 1970s resulted in greatly increased oil exports and rapid increases in export earnings. When it announced its debt-servicing difficulties, naturally the private commercial bank creditors of the developing countries were astonished.[44] They quickly reached the conclusion that, if Mexico could no longer service the debt, other developing countries must be in even more difficult situations.

Willingness to extend additional credits then virtually ceased. For many countries, capital inflows represented several percentage points of GDP and permitted expenditures in excess of income of equal magnitude. Even had there been no other economic problems, the sudden reduction in expenditures that would have been needed to accommodate the shift in net capital inflows would have created severe macroeconomic difficulties for most of the indebted countries. In fact, interest rates were rising rapidly, the commodity terms of trade had fallen sharply, and, of course, the cost of imports for oil-importing countries had risen sharply.

The consequent difficulties of the developing countries were acute. In most, it was infeasible to maintain voluntary debt servicing, and

42. World Bank (1985, p. 24).
43. World Bank (1985, p. 24).
44. Mexico's rapid increase in oil-export earnings had been paralleled by rapidly rising government expenditures, so that the Mexican fiscal deficit—and hence the need for foreign financing—was rising at least as rapidly as oil-export earnings.

finance ministers in country after country felt compelled to approach the IMF for support with their foreign exchange and debt-servicing difficulties.[45]

At first, observers blamed the worldwide recession and the run-up in nominal interest rates for these difficulties. It was widely thought that once economic activity accelerated in the developed countries, the debt-servicing difficulties would diminish greatly.

Differential Responses of Different Groups of Developing Countries

But, notably, the East Asian NICs and a few other developing countries, including Turkey, were not forced to seek debt rescheduling. Indeed, the East Asian NICs experienced a year or two of reduced growth, but they adjusted fairly quickly and resumed their rapid growth. Analysis showed that the East Asian NICs had had approximately the same ratio of debt and debt-servicing obligations to GDP as had other oil-importing countries, but they also had far lower ratios of debt and debt-servicing obligations to exports.[46]

As the 1980s progressed, the lessons gradually became clearer. Borrowing to finance productive investment, as had been done in East Asia, generated earnings streams that enabled debt-servicing obligations to be met—though with difficulty during worldwide recession. But borrowing to avoid adjustment resulted in mounting debt-servicing obligations and trouble for the future.

Moreover, it became evident in retrospect that growth rates for most of the import-substitution-oriented developing countries had been falling,[47] or at least would have been falling, if external and deficit financing had not been used to shore up flagging growth rates accompanying underlying economic inefficiencies. By 1983, for example, the World Bank could report that developing countries had more than achieved their target rates of saving and investment that

45. See World Bank (1985, p. 28), for a listing of debt renegotiations between 1975 and 1984. In 1983, the number of debt reschedulings exceeded the cumulative total over the 1975–80 period.

46. See Sachs (1985).

47. An exception was China and the South Asian countries. There, growth rates had not earlier been very high, but financing had by and large been conservative so that growth continued largely unaffected by worldwide events. In retrospect, it became clear that the cost of this "insulation" from the world economy had been slow growth.

had been thought adequate to result in higher rates of economic growth.[48] However, despite those much higher rates of saving and investment, growth rates had not risen. At best, higher rates of investment had only offset rising incremental capital-output ratios, and in some countries growth rates had fallen sharply.[49]

Further analysis revealed that these rising capital-output ratios were symptomatic of the underlying difficulties with development strategies that were based on import substitution and government controls over the economy. Government controls and state-owned enterprises had resulted in cumbersome and economically inefficient activities, which incurred large deficits. Financing those deficits was one of the causes of mounting financing requirements from foreign countries.

Why An Import-Substitution Strategy Cannot Sustain Growth

It took the debt crisis to convince many policymakers and economists of the inherent difficulties of reliance on import-substitution as a growth strategy. Not only are there reasons—cited above—to believe that an outer-oriented trade strategy offers prospects of better economic performance, compelling considerations suggest that growth under import substitution is bound to slow down and cannot be sustained.

To open their economies and achieve economic growth developing countries must recognize the flaws in the import-substitution strategy. And growth strategies that rely on an outer orientation depend in part on an international economy that provides market access for goods from developing countries.[50]

48. World Bank (1983, chap. 3).

49. It may be objected that the neoclassical growth model would project that a rising rate of investment would normally encounter diminishing returns to additional capital formation, and that this could have accounted for slower growth. But incremental capital-output ratios in many developing countries—India, for example—rose to levels well above those prevailing in developed countries. It was simply not plausible that, at the low levels of capital per person that prevailed, economically efficient capital-deepening accounted for the phenomenon.

50. Even if market access were severely restricted, those developing countries that maintained outer-oriented trade strategies would fare better than those that attempted to insulate themselves from the world economy. But "faring better" would be to experience much less satisfactory growth performance than would be achievable with reasonable market access.

Import substitution began easily, but over time the problems with the strategy mounted.[51] Obviously, import-substitution policies had initially encouraged the establishment and expansion of the industries in which comparative disadvantage was least: these were industries, such as textiles, apparel, and footwear, intensive in the use of un-skilled labor, with a sizable domestic market, and in which capital investment per unit of output was relatively low.

Once the "easy" opportunities for import substitution were largely exhausted, the new candidates normally had higher capital-labor ratios than the old, while simultaneously, many of the goods were items demanded by only the few in the upper-income groups in poor countries.[52] This phenomenon had two effects, both deleterious for growth. On one hand, the higher capital-labor ratios entailed meant that a higher rate of saving and investment would be needed to maintain the rate of economic growth. On the other hand, for those industries, probably the majority, with fixed costs and a minimum efficient scale of production, the cost disadvantages of producing in developing countries for small domestic markets were significant. The greater the minimum efficient size of plant relative to the size of the domestic market, and the greater were fixed costs, the greater these cost disadvantages were. For most developing countries, domestic markets were small not only because domestic populations were small but also because incomes were so low that little was left for purchasing commodities other than basic consumer goods.[53]

51. Import-substitution strategies also resulted in the emergence of groups with strong interests in the perpetuation of policies. Political opposition to altering strategy was therefore strong and accounts for some of the problems developing countries have had in changing policies since the debt crisis. That phenomenon, though of great importance for understanding difficulties with policy reform, is not central to the issues under consideration here. See Bates and Krueger (1993) for a discussion.

52. Many of these later import-substitution industries were ones where skilled technicians were an integral part of economically efficient production processes. In many developing countries, there were few qualified people. One of the consequences was the very low quality of production of many items, as firms could not afford to hire the scientists, engineers, and technicians who could (with the appropriate capital equipment) have provided quality control.

53. A calculation undertaken by the author (Krueger, 1984, p. 145) in the early 1980s indicated that the size of the domestic market for *all* manufactured goods in India and Brazil—the two developing countries with the then-largest markets—was about the same size as that of Sweden. For many developing countries, with populations less than 10 million, the inefficiencies of import substitution because of size alone are highly significant.

These disadvantages would have caused difficulties, reflected in a rising incremental capital-output ratio, as import-substitution policies continued. But another major, and initially underestimated, difficulty quickly arose: once protection from imports was almost automatic, domestic import-substituting producers were provided with monopoly positions in the sheltered domestic market. The incentives given—usually prohibition of imports once domestic production was deemed of an adequate size—were so great that few producers found it worthwhile to enter markets in which production had already started. It was far simpler and more assuredly profitable to identify commodities from the import list not yet domestically produced and to begin production of new items.

Thus, even when there might have been sufficient cost advantage to enable domestic producers to cover their costs and export, it seldom made sense for them to expand for the export market. Profitability was assured, probably including monopoly profits, with entry into new lines for the domestic market.[54]

Moreover, in countries following import-substitution strategies, a genuine conflict occurs. Multiple producers of an item usually result in smaller-scale plants for each producer, which increases the economic costs of less-than-efficient size. The authorities are thus caught between the desirability of assuring competition and the high costs of small production runs in small markets.

Finally, several conditions contributed to the periodic foreign exchange crises that occurred in developing countries. It was automatically more profitable and easier for them to seek new import-substitution items than to expand capacity to begin exporting. The developing countries experienced a higher-than-anticipated demand for imports arising from import-substitution activities, and they did not focus on incentives for export growth. Thus, vulnerability from the consequences of import substitution, not exogenous events from the rest of the world, led to foreign exchange crises.[55]

54. It will be recalled that nominal exchange rates were often held fixed for long periods during inflation. Incentives for exporting were so severely neglected in many countries following policies of import substitution that it was often not possible for most producers of nontraditional items even to cover marginal costs of production except in periods immediately after devaluation. The only viable exports were those where there were sizable rents accruing to minerals or agricultural commodities. Even then, incentives often resulted in a neglect of maintenance expenditures in mines and lack of investment in agriculture.

55. Many crises nonetheless came about during periods of worldwide recession. This synchronicity is not inconsistent with the proposition that import-substitution policies gen-

Although import substitution has other drawbacks, these considerations highlight the importance for developing countries of relying on the international market as they grow. Although import-substitution policies may yield satisfactory growth initially, they cannot be sustained indefinitely except at very high cost and usually with a declining rate of economic growth.

That lesson is being learned. For developing countries, import substitution is not a viable development strategy. Reliance on an outer-oriented trade policy and integration with the international economy is. Such a strategy is likely to lead to a preferred developmental outcome in all but the worst-case scenarios for the international economy. However, the ability of political leaders to adopt such a strategy, and the extent to which it results in more satisfactory economic performance, is very much a function of the health and growth of the international economy.

---

erated the vulnerability: had incentives for exports been greater, and those for import substitution less, countries would have been in a better position to manage downturns in the international economy. The experience of the East Asian NICs and other countries that have altered policies attests to that.

Chapter 2

The Role of the Developing Countries in the International Economy

D URING THE 1980s and early 1990s, many developing countries not only reversed their own economic policies, but as discussed in chapter 1, sought to change their role in GATT and the world trading system from that of "free rider" to active participant.

As part of that shift, developing countries bargained actively during the Uruguay Round. They yielded "concessions" on several issues of concern, but they also achieved some major benefits. Because of these events, developing countries have already become committed to taking steps that will result in deeper integration.

Relations with GATT and the World Trading System until the 1980s

The suspicion with which the leaders of developing countries viewed the international economy in the 1950s and 1960s has already been noted. In part, that suspicion originated in bitter memories of the colonial experience and the belief that the colonial powers had used their political power to extract wealth from the colonies to the detriment of the colonies and the benefit of the home countries. In part, however, rejection of immediate integration with the global economy was based on the infant industry argument and the view that industrialization could not be undertaken without insulation from competition from established foreign industries.

Because of these views and the fact that the developing countries were using restrictionist trade and payments regimes to insulate themselves from the world economy, the leaders of those countries did not believe they had a significant stake in the international trading system.[1] Further, they believed that the "rules of the game" under GATT were inappropriate for them.

The Balance-of-Payments Exception in the GATT Articles

The initial GATT articles already recognized some of these concerns. Later, at the insistence of developing countries, the articles were amended.[2] The overall thrust was that developing countries were accorded "special and differential treatment" within GATT. There were three aspects. One, developing countries did not undertake the same obligations as developed countries within GATT. As a part of differential obligations, developing countries benefited from whatever tariff reductions developed countries negotiated among themselves in multilateral tariff negotiations. Because of the entitlement of the developing countries to most favored nation treatment, they were not obligated to offer any reciprocal reductions. Two, developing countries were treated preferentially with respect to GATT codes. Finally, unlike developed countries, developing countries were permitted to enter into preferential trading arrangements without going all the way to zero tariff rates. This third provision has had little practical importance and is not further dealt with here.

In the GATT articles themselves, article XVIII was intended to provide developing countries with differential treatment. This article contained three sections, of which section B as amended proved to be the one used by developing countries who wished to protect their

1. To be sure, it was recognized that foreign exchange earnings would be essential to finance the imports of goods deemed essential for the development program. It was thought, however, that the industrialization process would result in the replacement of imports over time and hence reduced reliance on the international economy. It was hoped, if not expected, that foreign aid would finance many of the needed capital goods imports. The time period during which it was thought that domestic availability of import-competing goods would be established was not at all clear.

2. More accurately, the articles were amended several times to take into account the concerns of the developing countries. There was even an added part IV, entitled "Trade and Development," although as pointed out by Dam (1970, pp. 91–94) this was more a statement of principles and intent than a change in the rules governing trade.

infant industries.[3] Article XVIII:B permitted the use of quantitative restrictions on imports by developing countries whenever a threat of balance-of-payments difficulties was perceived.[4]

As analyzed by Kenneth W. Dam,

Article XVIII was the principal provision in the General Agreement dealing directly with the trade problems of less-developed countries . . . Article XVIII reflected the predominance of the import substitution approach to economic development. . . . The theory of the article is quite simply that less-developed countries should be freer than developed countries to impose quantitative and other restrictions in order to protect infant industries and to combat payments imbalances.[5]

Because of the resort to article XVIII:B developing countries could simultaneously be members of GATT and employ the restrictive trade and exchange rate practices that they did. As pointed out by Brian Hindley, the ease with which developing countries could evade the obligation to eschew quantitative restrictions rendered any commitments they might have made to lower tariffs and bind them relatively meaningless.[6] They therefore had relatively little bargaining power in GATT rounds of multilateral tariff negotiations because their reciprocal "concessions" were of doubtful value.

3. Article XII was the original article that permitted quantitative restrictions in the event of balance-of-payments difficulties. However, it was tightened up by the mid-1950s. Thereafter, developing countries resorted to article XVIII:B, which had less stringent standards for developing countries' use of quantitative restrictions (including less frequent surveillance of the use of quantitative restrictions than was required for developed countries with similar trade restrictions).

4. Dam (1970, pp. 227–28). Dam notes that the third section of the same article permits the imposition of quantitative restrictions "where required to promote the establishment of a particular industry with a view to raising the general standard of living." (p. 228). This provision was obviously intended to enable infant industry protection (via quantitative restrictions). However, developing countries preferred to use the balance-of-payments justification, so section C was not used.

5. Dam (1970, p. 227).

6. Hindley (1987). Tariff "binding" is the procedure used in GATT in rounds of multilateral tariff negotiations. Exchanges of tariff reductions would be meaningless if countries could afterward at their discretion again raise tariffs. Hence, tariffs are "bound" by agreement once the agreed-upon concessions are ratified. Countries may unilaterally lower tariffs below their bound level, but they may not raise them above it except in cases of "serious injury" and, even then, "compensation" in the form of other concessions must be given.

At the start of the Uruguay Round, it was estimated that only 22 percent of tariffs in developing countries were bound under GATT rules contrasted with 78 percent of developed countries' tariffs (see note 25). Since there was ample scope to raise tariffs unilaterally under GATT rules, not surprisingly developed countries' negotiators did not value promised additional tariff cuts.

Generalized System of Preferences

In the 1950s and 1960s, developing countries campaigned for preferential treatment vis-à-vis developed countries in addition to their exemption from GATT obligations. This effort led to a series of changes in GATT provisions, including the new part IV. Finally, in the mid-1970s, the developed countries acceded still further to developing countries' pressures and agreed to a Generalized System of Preference (GSP). Under GSP, individual developed countries were enabled, despite the most favored nation clause in the GATT articles, to provide for preferential treatment for imports of specified goods from developing countries. This entitlement, when granted, in effect meant that developing countries' imports could enter developed country markets at a lower rate of duty than could comparable commodities imported from developed country sources.

GSP was a major derogation of the GATT principles of an open multilateral trading system, especially of the most favored nation principle.[7] The lessons of the 1980s and the consequent recognition of the importance of the multilateral trading system for developing countries argue strongly that GSP treatment was not in the long-term interests of developing countries.

Most analysts believe that, although GSP had some value to developing countries, it was limited to a few countries and a few commodities.[8] It may not have been worth even the diplomatic efforts and other costs to developing countries.

One reason for the relatively small value of GSP was that each developed country set its own rules for eligibility for GSP treatment

7. See the comments of Dam (1970, p. 247), written prior to the adoption of GSP. Dam commented that the "movement" that "most threatens the traditional GATT system is the widespread interest in a system of preferences for less-developed countries."

8. See the analysis and estimates in Baldwin and Murray (1977), and analyses of the effects of GSP in Frank (1979) and especially Wolf (1987).

and generally limited the quantities of imports that could enter at low duties. Sensitive items, such as textiles and apparel, were not accorded preferential status at all.

Furthermore, the few developing countries—the Asian NICs—whose outer-oriented trade policies made them competitive in international markets were the ones receiving most of the "preferences," and their value to the less advanced developing countries was limited. Estimates by Guy Karsenty and Sam Laird show that three countries (Hong Kong, South Korea, and Taiwan) received 44 percent of the total gains from GSP tariff reductions and that other countries received proportionately much less benefit.[9]

Once advanced developing countries had succeeded in increasing their exports to developed countries, developed countries' governments were free to, and did, reduce or remove GSP: there was no equivalent to "binding" of tariffs under GSP. Indeed, as the following discussion of graduation suggests, it would be natural for any special and differential treatment to be withdrawn after a country has achieved a certain stage of development.[10] Whether developing countries' exporters should or would base their expansion plans too heavily on GSP, when GSP privileges are "artificial" and cannot be expected to be a source of more permanent comparative advantage, is open to question.

Finally, the relatively small value of GSP treatment was that tariff rates on most industrial products among the developed countries were already very low and falling. Yet those declines were beneficial for developing countries, especially in light of the considerations already mentioned. Robert E. Baldwin and Tracy Murray estimated that the erosion of the value of GSP associated with a 50 percent across-the-board MFN tariff cut by the United States, Japan, and the European Community would on net benefit developing countries.[11]

9. The United States, for example, did not grant GSP treatment for imports of most textiles and apparel or for a number of other sensitive commodities. Even for commodities for which GSP treatment was granted, there was usually a limit of $25 million placed on imports that could qualify in each category. Karsenty and Laird (1987, p. 271).

10. Once GSP was established, it was natural of course for there to be disputes about the stage of development that should be achieved before it was removed. See the discussion of graduation below.

11. Baldwin and Murray (1977). Developing countries, once having attained preferential access through GSP, were reluctant to lose it and hence became much less enthusiastic supporters of multilateral tariff reductions than they otherwise would have been. Any reduction in tariff rates was seen as eroding their margin of preference.

If, instead of using such bargaining power as they had for GSP, developing countries had sought lower tariffs and fewer restrictions on developed countries' imports of goods from developing countries, the beneficial impact of even small reductions in tariffs of interest to developing countries would probably have exceeded that from GSP.

These difficulties with GSP seem inherent in the working of a preferential system. Since GSP preferences are not "bound" and can be altered by law—in commodity and in country coverage—by each country granting them, their value is inherently limited. That each developing country has relatively little bargaining power vis-à-vis any one developed country further limits their value. Most developing countries seem to have recognized their interest in a multilateral system, and support for GSP seems to have diminished.

Declining Importance in World Trade until the 1980s

While the developing countries were availing themselves of article XVIII:B to maintain quantitative restrictions, developed countries were liberalizing their trade under successive rounds of multilateral trade negotiations and moves toward currency convertibility. As a consequence of these contrasting trends, the developing countries became less and less important in world trade.

Even highly aggregated data tell the story. Table 2-1 gives data on world exports of manufactures and agricultural commodities and then provides a breakdown of sources of exports. The developed countries' share of manufactured exports remained approximately constant from 1955—83 percent of total world exports of manufactures—until 1980, while developing countries' share even fell until the mid-1970s.[12] Their share of exports of agricultural goods fell dramatically during the same period: from 44 percent of world exports of agricultural products in 1955 to 28 percent in 1980.

The Reversal and Increasing Importance of Developing Countries

The success of the East Asian countries naturally increased their share of world trade in manufactures, though they were starting from a very low base. By the mid-1970s, developing countries' share of

12. The third group of countries, whose totals are not reported here, are the centrally planned economies.

Table 2-1. *Developing Countries' Shares of World Exports of Manufactures and Agricultural Commodities*

Year	World exports	Developed countries' exports	Developing countries' exports
	Manufactures (billions of U.S. dollars)		
1955	46	38 (83)	3 (7)
1960	70	58 (83)	4 (6)
1965	109	90 (83)	6 (6)
1970	202	169 (84)	7 (3)
1975	518	434 (84)	40 (8)
1980	1,135	937 (83)	110 (10)
1985	1,221	956 (78)	167 (14)
1990	1,931	1,518 (79)	354 (18)
	Agricultural commodities (billions of U.S. dollars)		
1955	18	9 (50)	8 (44)
1960	22	12 (55)	8 (36)
1965	31	18 (58)	10 (32)
1970	41	24 (59)	13 (32)
1975	104	66 (63)	30 (29)
1980	200	130 (65)	56 (28)
1985	177	110 (62)	55 (31)
1990[a]	233	147 (63)	70 (30)

Sources: For 1955 to 1965, author's calculations based on data provided by UN Conference on Trade and Development; for 1970–85, UN Statistical Office Department of International Economic and Social Affairs; and for 1990 GATT (1992).

a. GATT data for agricultural trade for 1990 do not appear comparable with those estimates provided for earlier years. Data were therefore extrapolated by the author.

world exports of manufactures was beginning to increase, reaching 8 percent in 1975, (contrasted with 7 percent in 1955 and 3 percent in 1970 (see table 2-1). By 1980, developing countries' share of world trade in manufactures had risen to 10 percent, and by 1990, developing countries accounted for 18 percent of all world exports of manufactures.

These aggregate numbers fail to reveal the extent to which a few developing countries, especially those in East Asia, accounted for the reversal, especially prior to the mid-1980s. Nonetheless, they illustrate dramatically the consequences for the developing countries of their inner-oriented trade policies. Not only did developing countries lose shares of world markets for agricultural commodities, but even for manufactures—supposedly their leading growth sector—the growth of exports failed to keep pace with overall growth of world trade in manufactures.

The increase in the share of developing countries in trade in manufactures was accompanied by a small increase in the share of agricultural commodities that, in any event, had not fallen below a quarter of world agricultural trade. By the 1990s, some developing countries were already sufficiently large exporters that it was essential to include them in trading arrangements. Moreover, as other developing countries were altering their policies, there was every prospect that the importance of developing countries in world trade would increase.

Developed Countries' Trade Policies and Developing Countries

Any effort to analyze prospects for deeper integration between developed and developing countries must weigh proposals according to their impact on the economic efficiency of the world trading system.[13] Moreover, if developing countries are to be asked to undertake deeper integration at a cost to themselves, they will require assurances that protectionism will not thwart whatever benefits they might otherwise achieve in return for accepting premature (from the viewpoint of their development) deeper integration.

Two aspects must be considered. The first is the degree and forms of protectionism that are currently applied by industrial countries to imports from developing countries. The second, explored in chapter 3, is the extent to which calls for deeper integration might be disguised efforts to institute new forms of protectionism.

Even as developing countries placed protectionist barriers around their own markets in the 1950s and 1960s, developing countries were nonetheless benefiting from the expansion of the world economy. And, the NICs were enormously successful in penetrating developed countries' markets in the 1970s and 1980s.

However, when opening up of their economies was suggested to leaders of most of the developing countries following import-substitution policies in the era prior to the debt crisis, one of their stated

13. For a more complete survey of developed countries' trade barriers to developing countries' exports, see Grilli (1990).

concerns was that expansion of export supply would meet sufficiently protectionist responses in developed countries to thwart the effort.

Indeed, considerable protectionist sentiment prevails in developed countries, as evidenced by the concerns expressed by Ross Perot and others over "the great sucking sound" of the North American Free Trade Agreement (NAFTA), and by measures taken to restrict developing countries' exports to developed countries. Several trade restrictions applied by developed countries have been aimed at developing countries' exports, and most estimates of the restrictiveness of industrial countries' trade regimes have provided evidence that the industrial countries are on average more protectionist toward developing countries than they are toward one another.

Moreover, as growth of developed countries slowed down in the 1970s and 1980s, protectionist sentiment in developed countries, especially against the import of labor-intensive goods from developing countries, increased. It was noted that, as early as 1958, the Haberler report concluded that part of the failure of developing countries to increase exports had been protectionism in developed countries. In the mid-1960s, Harry Johnson summarized the situation well:

> In an important sense the trade policies of the developed countries may be said to discriminate against the less developed countries. While they generally do not discriminate against those countries in the form proscribed by the most-favored-nation principle, . . . their policies are in effect discriminatory in that the most serious barriers are erected against goods which the less developed countries typically have a comparative advantage in producing—agricultural commodities in raw or processed form, and labor-intensive, technologically unsophisticated consumer goods.[14]

Although a number of relatively high tariffs and voluntary export restraints (VERs) are placed on imports from developing countries, the most restrictive arrangements have been in textiles and apparel and in agriculture. Since both of these are affected by the Uruguay Round, it is worthwhile to understand the impact of these practices on exports from developing countries, and only these two protectionist practices will be reviewed here. Over the years, however, there have

---

14. Johnson (1967, p. 79).

been voluntary export restraints on exports of several commodities such as footwear, television sets, and other items of special interest to developing countries. If proposals for deeper integration mean a cost for developing countries, they will accept only if they are assured that protectionist practices and measures do not prevent their gaining access to the markets of developed countries.

The Multifiber Arrangement

Starting in the mid-1950s with a "short-term" agreement on textiles with Japan, the United States and later other industrialized countries developed the Multifiber Arrangement (MFA). Under that arrangement, whose umbrella agreement has been negotiated under GATT, a quantitative limit is established for the growth of imports of textiles and apparel into industrialized countries.[15]

Within that overall limit, each participating developed country then has bargained individually with individual developing countries to establish quotas on the various categories of textile and apparel that may be exported. Under the Multifiber Arrangement, developed countries do not impose quotas on imports from other developed countries. Only the exports of developing countries are affected. As new exporters have achieved some success in selling their products in developed countries' markets, developed countries have insisted on negotiating VERs with those countries, thus reducing their potential gains from trade. When new products, such as those made of ramie in the 1980s, not previously subject to restraint have been introduced, trade negotiators have added those items to the list.

With these moves, the MFA became increasingly restrictive in both country and commodity coverage, and, until the Uruguay Round Agreement, apparently entrenched. Most analyses of the trade between developed and developing countries identified the MFA as the restrictive trade device that was most costly to consumers in developed countries and to producers in developing countries. Gary C. Hufbauer and Kimberly Ann Elliot recently estimated that for the United States the tariff equivalent of MFA quotas in 1990 was 48 percent for textiles and 23 percent for apparel. The resulting annual

15. The reader interested in an overview of the world textile and apparel industry can consult Keesing and Wolf (1980) and Anderson (1992).

welfare loss from the MFA to the United States alone was estimated to be $7,712 million for textiles and $894 million for apparel in that year.

Agriculture

Although the share of world agricultural exports that originate in developing countries has declined, there are still many developing countries whose exports consist predominantly of agricultural commodities. According to GATT, although only 13 percent of developing countries' exports are agricultural, more than half of all developing countries had more than 20 percent of total exports consisting of agricultural commodities.[16]

In many instances, those commodities are tropical agricultural products, for which developed countries' tariffs have constituted a significant impediment to expanded exports.[17] In addition, sugar—which can be produced in tropical and temperate climates—is perhaps the agricultural commodity in which intervention has most affected the international market. On one hand, the United States permits some imports at high (domestic) prices under quota, while simultaneously restricting imports greatly. On the other hand, because of U.S. and other industrialized countries' domestic programs, the world price for sugar is normally well below what it would be in the absence of interventions by industrialized countries' governments.[18]

Agricultural commodities produced in temperate climates are subject to a wider range of industrialized countries' interventions that serve as protection against imports. As governments in developed countries have protected their domestic industries, they have reduced their imports from the world market or begun exporting surpluses (at the high domestic support prices). The result is world prices far below those that would prevail in the absence of these practices.[19] For

16. Cited in Rodrik (1994, pp. 19, 9).
17. There is also preferential treatment extended by a group of importers to some exporting countries for tropical commodities. Perhaps the most complex and controversial arrangements surround the imports of bananas from the Caribbean countries and from countries signatory to the Lome convention.
18. See the analyses in Marks and Maskus (1993).
19. See, for example, the analysis in Zietz and Valdés (1993). See also World Bank (1986).

exporters of temperate climate crops, the resulting low world prices are harmful.[20]

The Uruguay Round and the Developing Countries

As already noted, throughout most of the first four decades of GATT's existence, developing countries remained bystanders in successive rounds of trade negotiations. They also insisted on "special and differential treatment" and, to the extent they participated in negotiations at all, they sought to increase the scope of preferences.[21]

As world trade grew, so did markets for products from developing countries. Developing countries certainly benefited from the rapid expansion of the international economy, although their share of world trade fell as import-substitution policies pulled resources toward import-competing and away from exportable activities (see table 2-1). As developed countries were reducing their tariff rates after multilateral negotiations, developing countries benefited without undertaking to reduce their own protective structures. Indeed, it can even be argued that the liberalization of developed countries' trade and the favorable environment created by the growth of the international economy permitted some of the developing countries to maintain import-substitution development strategies as long as they did.

When, in the 1980s, recognition in developing countries grew that these policies had failed, attitudes toward GATT changed as well.[22] Especially among those developing countries that were further down

20. Many developing countries have, however, discriminated against their own agricultural producers so severely that agricultural products that might in an efficient allocation of resources be exported are imported. In many countries, policy reform has entailed significantly higher prices to producers of exportable commodities in many developing countries and encouraged increased output and exports. See Schiff and Valdes (1990). It should be recalled, as well, that some developing countries (most notably North Africa) are net importers of temperate agricultural commodities and would lose by having to face rising world prices for their imported goods.

21. Developing countries also pushed, under the United Nations Commission on Trade and Development, for commodity price stabilization agreements. Since that issue is not relevant for analysis of the developing countries' potential entry into arrangements for deeper integration, it is not discussed here.

22. The increased importance of developing countries—and especially the NICs—in world trade was also important in leading the developed countries to increase their resistance to the developing countries' "free riding" and remaining outside the system.

the path of policy reform and shifting to a more outer-oriented set of trade policies, a much greater willingness to support the open multilateral system and an increased recognition of their stake in that system took place.

At the same time, the success of the Asian NICs and the rapid entry of exports from other developing countries had increased the share of developing countries in trade, especially in manufactures, to levels that could no longer be ignored.[23] Trade representatives from developed countries were thus anxious to bring the developing countries into the Uruguay Round negotiations and to find means to bring developing countries more fully under GATT discipline.

Simultaneously, some policymakers in developing countries, having liberalized their trade regimes, recognized the importance of participating fully in the Uruguay Round. For the first time, the developing countries sought to influence the outcome of the Uruguay Round, rather than awaiting reciprocal tariff reductions among developed countries and free riding on those reductions.

As a result, the developing countries became much more active participants in the GATT round of trade negotiations, named the Uruguay Round, for that reason. The results of the round reflect the developing countries' pursuit of their interests in the negotiations and their increased influence and importance. Some of the agreements offer the prospect of far greater market access for the products of developing countries.

There are many parts of the Uruguay Round agreement that already promise to integrate more closely the developing countries into the World Trade Organization/GATT and oblige them to accept WTO/GATT disciplines. For many parts of the agreement, differential timetables exist for implementation by developed countries, developing countries, and "least developed countries." This latter group, as will be seen, has much longer periods for implementing agreements. It consists of countries with very low per capita incomes. The longer

---

23. According to UN (1990, p. 90) estimates, developing countries accounted for 15 percent of world exports of manufactures, 25 percent of mineral exports, and 22 percent of raw agricultural exports in 1987, the year the Uruguay Round was beginning. Many agricultural exports were, however, tropical products and were not competitive with most developed countries' agriculture. Mining, too, was less sensitive.

time permitted for implementation is to expire if their per capita income reaches $1,000.

Phaseout of Quantitative Restrictions and "Tariffication"

First of all, the Uruguay Round commits all countries, except the least developed, to phase out all quantitative restrictions.[24] This includes not only QRs on industrial goods but also QRs or other restrictions on agricultural imports, which must be "tariffied."

Eliminating their own remaining quantitative restrictions has already been demonstrated to yield positive results for developing countries, so that there is no cost to their adherence to the agreement. Removal of quantitative restrictions has already been accomplished in many developing countries and is under way in others. It is a necessary step in the process of policy reform. The least developed countries are given a longer period in which to achieve the tariffication of remaining trade barriers, but all GATT signatories will be obligated to eschew the use of quantitative restrictions after a transition period.

Of less immediate importance, but of potentially equal significance over the longer run, developing and developed countries are obligated to "bind" their tariffs to a much greater extent than they have done historically. Estimates show that only 22 percent of developing countries' industrial tariff lines had been bound pre-Uruguay, with only 14 percent of industrial imports coming in under bound tariffs. These numbers change to 72 percent and 59 percent respectively under the Uruguay Round agreement.[25]

But developed countries, too, are obliged to remove existing quantitative restrictions and refrain from future resort to them. This latter aspect means that voluntary export restraints can no longer be negotiated between developed and developing countries and, as such, provides assurances for developing countries that those measures cannot be used to restrict market access. But the proscription against quantitative restrictions also has important implications and benefits

24. There is still a balance-of-payments exception to the requirement that quantitative restrictions be eliminated, but the conditions under which it may be invoked are far more stringent than they have been heretofore, and those countries using it will be subject to more frequent and critical surveillance.

25. Rodrik (1994, pp. 11–12). The percentage of tariffs bound in developed countries is significantly higher. For the United States, it is almost 100 percent; for Western Europe, it is around 80 percent.

for developing countries because it implies the dismantling of the Multifiber Arrangement and a great liberalization of trade in agricultural commodities.

Phaseout of the Multifiber Arrangement

The Uruguay Round agreement calls for the phaseout of the Multifiber Arrangement and a removal of all quotas over ten years. Even during that time, the rate at which quotas are to be expanded is greatly increased. The phaseout is "backloaded" in the sense that almost half of the quantitative restrictions are to be removed only at the end of the transition period. However, the increases in quotas in the intervening period should result in their reduced restrictiveness so that phaseout, when it comes, will be far less dramatic than it would be were it to occur under existing MFA restrictions. For example, the annual rate of growth of import quotas over the 1995–1998 period is set to be 16 percent higher than the rate of growth in 1994. The rate of increase in quotas is then scheduled to increase to 25 percent in 1998, and 27 percent between 2002 and 2004. On January 1, 1995, each country was to remove quotas on at least 16 percent of its 1990 level of imports of textiles and apparel; three years later, quotas on another 17 percent must be eliminated, with another 18 percent being removed in 2002. According to some estimates world trade in textiles and apparel may increase by as much as 34 to 60 percent once the MFA phaseout is completed.[26]

Agriculture

The Uruguay Round agreement also calls for measures that will greatly liberalize trade in agricultural commodities benefiting, among others, developing countries that are net exporters. The agreement calls for an average reduction in tariffs and tariff-equivalents by 37 percent for imports of agricultural commodities. For exports of tropical agricultural products, the cut in subsidies is even higher—43 percent. In both cases, these new levels are to be bound.

Moreover, export subsidies and government budgetary support for agriculture is to be reduced by 36 percent for developed countries and 24 percent for developing countries. The volume of subsidized

26. Deardorff (1994, p. 19).

exports is to be reduced by 21 percent for developed countries and 14 percent for developing countries.

Like quantitative restrictions on industrial commodities, measures are also to be taken to make the supports more transparent and to replace quantitative restrictions with tariffs (which are then to be included in the schedule of reductions cited above).

Although the agreement on agriculture reduced agricultural protection in developed countries by less than the developing countries and some developed countries had originally hoped, it nonetheless represents a significant change in prospects for agricultural protectionism. Trade in agricultural commodities is now clearly under the aegis of WTO/GATT. Moreover, there are commitments to reduce the scope of intervention in the industrialized countries in ways that should redound to the benefit of the developing countries that export agricultural commodities. Alan V. Deardorff estimates that world trade in agricultural commodities should increase by around 20 percent once the phase-in period is completed.[27]

Intellectual Property Rights

Many developing countries have had weak or nonexistent intellectual property rights laws. Use of trademarks, patents, and copyrights, without permission or payment of licensing or royalty fees, has been common in many developing countries. The developed countries were insistent, during the Uruguay Round, that developing countries should adopt appropriate protection for intellectual property rights.

The Uruguay Round agreement stipulates that all signatories will adopt intellectual property rights protection in seven areas.[28] For patents, members of GATT are to implement legislation providing at least twenty years of protection. Developing countries will have longer to implement the agreement than developed countries. Most developing countries will have five years in which to bring their legislation into conformity with these provisions, in contrast to one year for developed countries.[29]

27. Deardorff (1994, p. 19).
28. These are copyrights, trademarks, geographical indications, industrial designs, layout designs of integrated circuits, patents, and undisclosed information.
29. Least developed countries have eleven years to implement the trade-related intellectual property rights agreement (TRIPs) and seven years for trade-related invest-

An inherent tension exists in the principles of economic efficiency when it comes to arrangements governing the investment in knowledge that is required for developing new items. On one hand, discovering, inventing, or creating new things is a private economic activity. To induce people to undertake research and development activities, write a book, or provide assurances of quality, they must have some assurance that they can recoup their expenses with an adequate rate of return. Development of new ideas and processes is a private good in production.

However, once an idea or process has been developed, the marginal cost of an additional use of the idea or process is zero. Efficient allocation of existing knowledge and technology would be achieved by permitting access to it without charge. However, such an allocation would immediately strongly deter any additional research and development.

Thus, a tension exists between achieving maximal benefits out of existing knowledge and achieving economic growth through the development of new knowledge and processes. When the developing countries adopt intellectual property laws consistent with the Uruguay Round agreement, some may lose in the short run by paying higher prices for drugs, reprinting rights for books, and other intellectual property.[30] The East Asian NICs are far enough advanced that they may immediately benefit through stronger intellectual property laws as additional research and development activity may be stimulated in their economies. Even developing countries with short-run losses will obtain some longer-term gains. The greater payoff to additional research and development that comes from better protection of intellectual property rights may be expected to induce the allocation of additional resources to it and a faster rate of technical development.

Nonetheless, it cannot be doubted that for some developing countries, and especially the poorer ones, the immediate costs of the

---

ment measures (TRIMs). There is also a provision for all developing countries that, for items that are not protected by patents at the end of the five-year period, another five years may be taken in implementing the protection.

30. Rodrik cites an estimate of the cost of IPR protection provided by Subramanian. Subramanian compared the cost of pharmaceuticals in Malaysia, where IPR protection is fairly strict, with the same drugs in India, where it is fairly lax. He found that Malaysian prices ranged from 17 to 767 percent above those in India. Rodrik notes that, besides the direct cost of higher prices, developing countries will be financing the foreign exchange cost of the larger royalty payments. Rodrik (1994, p. 16).

adoption of intellectual property rights law may be significant (although a substantial phase-in period exists for countries without such law, especially for the least developed countries). There are also questions about the administrative capacity of some of the developing countries to enforce intellectual property rights laws. To the extent that scarce administrative resources are allocated to enforcement of those laws, rather than tax reform, improvements in agricultural research and extension services, or more efficient administration of infrastructure investments, the costs to some developing countries may be even higher than a direct estimate of the cost of royalty or licensing fees would suggest.

Nonetheless, in light of the gains that developing countries made in terms of the MFA and agriculture, the short-term costs of intellectual property rights protection are probably worth incurring. In the longer term, of course, those who wish to witness sustained development in their countries would eventually need to implement intellectual property laws.

Trade-Related Investment Measures

Another subject on which the developed countries insisted agreement should be reached was trade-related investment measures (TRIMs). Here, their concern was with the conditions that have been placed by many developing countries on multinational firms investing in their countries. It has not been uncommon to require exports of a certain percentage of output, or the use of a specified percentage of domestic components, as a precondition for permitting foreign investment.

Under the TRIMs agreement, performance requirements such as local-content, links between imports and exports, and export targets are to be phased out as permissible conditions on investment for domestic and foreign firms.[31] Developing countries are given five years to remove performance requirements, in contrast with two years for developed countries.

Unlike the TRIPs agreement, where there are short-run costs for adherence for some developing countries, the TRIMS agreement

31. The agreement rules these requirements out for both domestic and foreign investment. However, these requirements have been much more widely imposed on foreign investors in the past and therefore will have more of an effect on foreign investment than domestic in most cases.

basically calls for countries to refrain from adopting policies that would be economically inefficient. In that sense, except for whatever transition costs there are, the impact on developing countries of adherence to TRIMs should be almost entirely positive.[32]

Trade in Services

As transport and communications costs and times have declined, trade in services has become more important relative to trade in goods. Another major accomplishment of the Uruguay Round was to achieve agreement that trade in services would be brought under multilateral trade disciplines in the World Trade Organization.

Initially, the developed countries pushed for inclusion of trade in services under a multilateral discipline. The developing countries were highly resistant. Over time, however, that resistance diminished and finally was largely overcome, as it came to be recognized that they probably held a significant comparative advantage in many services, for example, construction, if only access to markets could be obtained.

Unlike trade in commodities, where tariffs, quantitative restrictions, and other border measures have been the predominant form of discrimination against foreign producers, the unique characteristics of each form of service—banking, insurance, movies, construction, professional services, and so on—mean that the forms of regulation that have discriminated against foreigners (sometimes unintentionally) have differed item by item. That means that negotiations over trade in services must largely be sector specific.

The only general principle that is to apply to all services is national treatment, which ensures that foreign firms cannot be discriminated against. By and large, the agreement provides an umbrella under which multilateral negotiations for improved access for service providers can be achieved multilaterally.[33] Members of GATS (the Gen-

32. The only real issue under TRIMs will be one of transition for already established firms. Some existing firms initially invested when their costs were conditioned by requirements to use domestic goods or submit to other cost-raising measures. Here, the major difficulty is that earlier investors, having paid higher investment costs than they would have had they had free access to the international market, may be at a disadvantage when they are competing with new entrants who are not so restricted. In some activities, such as auto assembly, this issue may be highly significant. In many lines of production, however, it is probably much more marginal.

33. For particulars see Hoekman (1994).

eral Agreement on Trade in Services) will all—developed and developing countries alike—be signatories to each negotiated services agreement, and each must submit lists of liberalization sectors and actions.[34] However, since the extent of liberalization and the subsectors to which it will apply are at the discretion of individual developing countries, it is not clear what the force of this provision will be.

There are many other provisions of WTO, but the ones described are the chief ones that already provide greater integration with the world economy for developing countries than prevailed earlier. Some of these provisions, such as improved dispute settlement procedures and changes in dumping and subsidy agreements, will improve the functioning of the international system, and not significantly affect trade policies and administration in developing countries. In some instances, such as intellectual property provisions, enforcement may prove challenging. Administrative apparatuses in some developing countries are likely to be challenged by the necessity for enforcement for reasons already noted. In other areas, such as the framework agreement for services, developing countries may not immediately be called upon to undertake significant changes in current practices. Over the longer run, however, pressures to accede to service codes will probably intensify.

Conclusions

The world is already witnessing the increasing integration of the developing countries into the international economy. Not only have developing countries unilaterally reduced their tariff barriers and liberalized their trade regimes, but their obligations under the Uruguay Round Agreement in the WTO will greatly exceed their obligations under GATT.

Many of these new obligations, such as elimination of quantitative restrictions, are very much in the interests of developing countries. They constitute part of what must be done to pursue an outer-oriented trade strategy. In many countries, these trade-liberalizing mea-

---

34. In earlier "codes," joining was not obligatory, and few developing countries signed most of them.

sures would have been undertaken even without an international agreement to do so. In other instances, however, there are beginnings of deeper integration. In some cases, such as patent protection for pharmaceuticals, additional costs will be imposed on developing countries as prices of drugs increase. To the developing countries, however, these costs were presumably deemed necessary as part of the bargain to gain increased access and reduced protectionism for several items of interest to developing countries.

As the Uruguay Round is implemented, much more integration of the developing countries into the international economy will already have taken place, as those already on the path of policy reform open up and liberalize their economies and as other countries embark on policy reform programs. However, the effects of proposals for deeper integration that go beyond the Uruguay Round agreement on the developing countries will also be important.

Chapter 3

The Impact of Deeper Integration

THE PROVISIONS of the Uruguay Round agreement call for actions on the part of the developing countries that will inevitably result in their deeper integration into the world economy. Some of these provisions, such as the phasing out of quantitative restrictions, may prove politically difficult for some countries but have been demonstrated to be necessary for satisfactory economic performance. Others, such as the implementation of protection for intellectual property rights, will entail costs in the short run to all but the most advanced developing countries. However, those arrangements were part of the bargain in return for which developing countries expect to gain a great deal by the dismantling of the Multifiber Agreement and other trade-liberalizing measures taken by the developed countries.

Taking as a given that the Uruguay Round provisions will be implemented as scheduled, what effects will proposals for still more measures for deeper integration have on developing countries?

Another question frequently raised is, are the developing countries that could, in principle, enter into arrangements for deeper integration capable of doing so? Finally, two particular issues raised by the prospect of deeper integration are very important to the developing countries: proposals for labor standards and proposals on links between trade and environmental protection.

Different Groups and Interests of Developing Countries

As discussed in chapter 1, in the 1950s and 1960s developing countries could be viewed as a broadly homogeneous group, at least in comparison with developed countries. Certainly, that was so with respect to the participation of developing countries in the international economy. They had formed a block to pursue their perceived interests in the international trading system and were almost unanimous as to what those interests were.

By the late 1970s, that homogeneity had already greatly diminished. The East Asian newly industrializing countries (NICs) were succeeding in their outer-oriented trade strategy and as such had a vital interest in their access to international markets and the healthy growth of the international economy.

Moreover, different groups of developing countries following import-substitution policies had achieved very different growth rates, resulting in a distinct group of middle-income countries and another group of low-income countries.[1]

Low-income countries by and large relied almost exclusively on exports of primary commodities and remained recipients of large inflows of official capital (much of it concessional assistance) as export earnings were stagnant or only growing slowly.[2] Sub-Saharan African countries in particular had experienced poor growth performance.

Many low-income countries had failed to realize enough growth to maintain per capita incomes constant.[3] Despite very small domestic markets, most had adopted highly interventionist economic policies with large parastatal sector enterprises undertaking new import-substitution activities and extremely restrictionist import regimes. Their economies had become more and more insulated from the world economy, with unrealistic exchange rates, a declining share of trade in GDP, and very poor overall economic performance.

1. See any of the data tables of the World Bank's *World Development Reports* to see the classification of countries into those categories.

2. The Asian subcontinent was once again a partial exception. Although the countries were all low income and among the world's poorest, the commodity composition of Indian, and to a lesser extent Pakistani, exports (which still represented an abnormally low percentage of GDP) had already shifted toward a much greater share for manufactured goods.

3. See World Bank (1982, pp. 20–30).

By the 1990s, middle-income countries included the successful outer-oriented Asian NICs, some countries still following import-substitution policies, and already some other countries—most notably Thailand, Malaysia, Chile, and Turkey—that were starting or in the process of shifting their trade and payments regime.

Some middle-income countries relying on import substitution as a growth strategy at least until the 1980s had achieved real rates of economic growth between 5 percent and 7 percent and had, despite the inner orientation of their trade policies, experienced some development of nontraditional exports. They were not as insulated from the world economy as others despite protectionist policies.[4] To be sure, they still advocated special treatment for developing countries in the international trading system and were generally experiencing declining shares of trade in gross domestic product (GDP).

As if the differences between low- and middle-income developing countries were not enough, there were also significant differences between and among oil-importing and oil-exporting developing countries. There were both low- and middle-income developing countries among the oil importers and the oil exporters. Generally, the middle- (and high-) income oil exporters were relatively unpopulous countries. The low-income countries among the oil exporters included more heavily populated countries (relative to their oil revenues) such as Egypt and Indonesia.

During the 1980s, diversity among developing countries and their interests in the international economy increased still further. Some developing countries continued or began rapid growth during the 1980s. Others experienced a "lost decade" as the impact of the worldwide recession and the debt crisis was not overcome.

Whereas such indicators as literacy rates, educational attainments, and life expectancy had been fairly similar (in contrast to the developed countries) in the 1950s and 1960s, disparities among developing countries were vast by the early 1990s. Countries such as Korea had population growth rates, levels of educational attainment, and life expectancies that were much closer to those of the developed countries than they were to those of other developing countries. At the

4. It is often suggested that those countries, such as Brazil and Argentina, were heavily dependent on the international economy even in the years they were following import-substitution policies. In a sense, most developing countries do not have a realistic option of withdrawing from the international economy.

other end of the spectrum, primary school enrollment rates had even fallen in several countries, and little or no progress had been made in reducing infant mortality or otherwise improving the quality of life.

Developing Countries and Deeper Integration

Whether developing countries may maintain market access without participating in future arrangements for deeper integration made by developing countries is open to question. Logically, two concerns arise. One, are developing countries able to undertake measures of deeper integration *if the benefits to them from maintaining access to the developed countries are sufficient to induce them to do so*? Two, are there ways in which deeper integration can be achieved to enhance growth prospects or, when deeper integration is costly, reduce the resulting deterioration in growth prospects?

Although these questions are interrelated, they are not the same. On one hand, some measures, such as intellectual property rights protection, may be judged as incurring at least some costs for developing countries in the short run, but those costs are not so large as to impair growth prospects. Hence they constitute a reasonable "price" for maintaining market access. On the other hand, there are possible measures, such as labor standards, that would cut off the gains from trade to developing countries in ways that would preclude their achieving the benefits from the international economy that they otherwise would.

All of the developing countries, those that have successfully made the transition to outer-oriented, middle-income NICs, those in the process of policy reform, and those still adhering to the older policy stance but experiencing unsatisfactory economic performance and thus confronting the necessity for policy reform, have a strong interest in a healthy and expanding international trading system. Whatever their economic policies, a prosperous international economy will enable more rapid growth than would a world economy in which markets grow slowly or protectionist pressures prevent market penetration. For countries with governments committed to changing economic policies, the health of the international economy is even more vital.

The ability of developing countries to adopt the measures necessary for deeper integration varies considerably, however. For those countries in which the reform process has not yet started or has barely begun, it makes little sense even to contemplate most measures of deeper integration until liberalization of the trade and payments regime is accomplished. Even for those that have achieved initial liberalization, there may be other things to do that are more pressing than taking the necessary steps for deeper integration, for example, further financial liberalization, achievement of article VIII convertibility on current account, or privatization of parastatals. For countries that have altered their policies and achieved ten or more years of steady growth, however, the capability to undertake deeper integration is much greater.

If developed countries should decide upon deeper integration in some facets of economic activity, they could provide time-phased "concessions" of different lengths to different groups of developing countries. If, for example, it were proposed to harmonize competition policy, perhaps those developed countries signatory to the competition code would have three years in which to alter their domestic legislation to make it conform to the agreed-upon policies, whereas NICs (defined by per capita income or some other suitable criterion) would have a five years—or perhaps even a little longer—in which to adapt.[5] Countries in the process of policy reform might, by contrast, be given ten or more years, while countries not yet having begun policy reform might be accorded twenty-five years.[6]

Such differential criteria would meet most of the objectives of the developed countries.[7] On one hand, economies that remain highly constrained by government policies are unlikely to constitute a serious competitive threat on world markets. On the other hand, developing countries that have not yet addressed fundamental questions of initiating policy reform are unlikely to be capable of introducing the necessary administrative and legal changes necessary for harmonization. If it were credible that, a number of years in the future, they

5. To use this example is not to imply that any or all groups of developing countries would benefit by such a harmonization.

6. In the absence of these policy reforms, there should be very little concern about "unfair" competition on the part of exporters from developing countries. In regimes where policy reform has not been undertaken, the "bias" against exporters is normally substantial, which is why export growth has generally been so unsatisfactory.

7. A possible exception is the People's Republic of China, where rapid export growth has been achieved with a large residue of government controls. See Shirk (1994) in this series for a discussion.

would have to conform or lose access to markets, that credibility in itself could contribute to the policy reform process.

Policy Reform and Constraints on Administrative Capacity

As seen in chapter 1, the underlying view of economic policy that drove the decision to rely on import substitution for economic growth also led to extensive government intervention in almost all spheres of economic activity. One of the results was a neglect of some traditional government functions as bureaucracies were stretched to their limits to perform the nontraditional economic roles demanded of them. Another result was the establishment of a series of large parastatal enterprises undertaking various economic activities that were traditionally associated with private sector production in the industrialized countries.

Over time, the costs of those interventions and "government failures" have become more obvious. Deficits of parastatal enterprises increased, as did their payrolls, without commensurate increases in output.

Ironically, one of the results of this overstretching of governmental capabilities has been the erosion of capacity for undertaking responsibilities efficiently. Yet the policy reform process demands actions on many fronts. Parastatal enterprise deficits must be reduced, and the enterprises themselves privatized (a difficult challenge) or reorganized to make them more efficient. Tax administration generally requires reorganization, often accompanied by reform of the tax structure. Earlier neglect of maintenance of infrastructure usually means that attention must be devoted to rehabilitating roads that have returned to jungle, silted ports, and various other items in the public capital stock. Price controls and other regulations over private economic activity must be removed. A desire to encourage private foreign investment usually leads to the need for a new regime governing foreign capital inflows. Financial deregulation is necessary. And, of course, the trade regime itself requires liberalization.

The problem for top officials intent upon policy reform is that not all of these things can be done at once. Many require preparation, which can entail the establishment of teams, the airing of different interests, and the use of lawyers and economists who can draft the appropriate decrees or proposed laws. For many issues, parliamentary approval is desirable and parliament can, and often does, need to be persuaded of the desirability of the proposed changes.

Moreover, many of the needed policy reforms are politically painful. Such reforms as laying off parastatal enterprise employees, removing price controls, or reducing the number of approvals necessary prior to investing (and therefore depriving some officials and expediters of their functions) may be crucial to the improved long-run performance of the economy, but they are not usually undertaken without political opposition.

Economic policymakers, therefore, are constantly choosing the priority targets for reform from the many items requiring change, and domestic policy considerations often constrain them in the rate at which they can move. For countries undergoing overall policy reform, therefore, one question about the desirability of taking the necessary steps for deeper integration must be the degree to which those steps would reduce the "political capital" with which policymakers could attempt to carry out other needed reforms.

Administrative Capacity

How and why bureaucratic apparatuses developed to administer import licenses must be dismantled is readily understood. It is also fairly easy to understand why opposition to abandoning import licensing is likely not only from those in charge of administering the system but also from those who worked the system as "expediters" and "facilitators."

Many citizens of advanced countries may find it difficult, however, to comprehend the challenges of developing relatively efficient and honest administrative apparatuses for legitimate and necessary functions such as tax collection. Yet, in most developing countries in which import substitution was adopted, government bureaucracies sprang up to undertake a number of "control" tasks such as investment licensing, price controls, and import licensing, to the neglect of many of the legitimate and necessary functions of government.

Policy reform is not, therefore, simply a process of changing one or two aspects of governmental regulations and behavior. It requires a fairly stringent reorientation of government agencies away from "control" and "policing" functions and toward provision of public services and a level playing field for private economic activity.

Achieving this reform of public services is a major part of the overall policy reform process and one of the most challenging and difficult. At the same time, in most developing countries, there is a relatively thin layer of highly competent and well-educated administrators at the top of the bureaucracy. Generally speaking, the number of top-level administrators and managers who can oversee the necessary reorganizations and reorientations of various parts of the bureaucracy is limited.

Thus the capacity for administrative reform and the development of new, more efficient, bureaucratic apparatuses are limited in many developing countries. As scarce administrative resources are directed toward one set of reforms, less can be done for any other set.

Indeed, in some instances, achieving the desired results seems to be virtually impossible. When those in charge of enforcing and collecting tax revenues, for example, are confronted with an agency of tax collectors who are accustomed to accepting bribes to accept returns that greatly underreport income, turning that agency into a lean, honest, and efficient tax-collecting enterprise becomes a great challenge. Reforming customs administration so that imports will be quickly and honestly processed with legal (and only legal) duties collected is also a challenge for any government.[8]

The lack of administrative capacity in some developing countries has important ramifications when one considers calls for deeper integration. Most types of deeper integration would require that the governments establish an appropriate bureaucratic apparatus for carrying out the designated function.[9] When top officials, despite firm resolve and good intentions, cannot significantly alter the behavior of many government agencies, there are grounds to question whether some of the kinds of deeper integration that are proposed could be carried out even if top officials were convinced they were urgent. In some instances, prior reforms may be necessary before it is even possible to contemplate addressing the issue of deeper integration.

One example, derived from concerns over intellectual property rights, may help make the argument more concrete. In many developing countries, such rights have been flagrantly violated by small

8. In the late 1980s the Mexican authorities finally dismissed all existing customs inspectors and hired and trained an entirely new cadre of collectors.

9. This would be true, for example, of environmental codes, labor standards, intellectual property right enforcement, and a host of other issues.

producers who copy brand name designs, place the brand name on their product, and sell in the secondary market. Often the "counter-feiters" are legitimately producing some of the product for the brand name designer under contract, but then they also produce an additional quantity for sale to buyers other than the designer or brand name holder.

Efforts to enforce copyright at early stages of development are fraught with difficulty. On one hand, if the agency charged with administration of the copyright is not adequately organized, "pirates" will very likely bribe officials to look the other way as they continue to market their product. On the other hand, if enforcement is overly zealous (especially when there is a history of heavy-handed government intervention), there are strong risks of discouraging exactly the sort of legitimate development of economic activity that reform is intended to encourage and that will eventually offer strong incentives to shift resources away from pirating to more profitable activities.

As policy reform proceeds and as the civil service is reorganized to carry out different functions, the capacity for enforcing copyrights, patents, intellectual property rights, and other agreements increases greatly.

Advanced Developing Countries and Deeper Integration

Many observers have questioned the ability, even of advanced developing countries, to successfully join customs unions or common markets with industrialized countries. The issue was posed during the debate on the North American Free Trade Agreement (NAFTA) and had earlier arisen when the full membership of Spain and Portugal in the European Union was under consideration.

Fortunately, by now some evidence from Spain and Portugal, as well as from other entities such as Hong Kong and Puerto Rico, can allay those concerns.[10]

10. It is well known that Puerto Rico has experienced economic difficulties. Nonetheless, Puerto Rican per capita income has been several times that of most other Latin American countries, and its integration with the mainland has surely been a significant factor in accounting for the difference. Puerto Rico's "special circumstances," however, have included factor (including labor) mobility with the mainland, as well as tax advantages.

Experience of Now-Advanced Developing Countries

Consideration is therefore confined initially to the groups of countries that were earlier identified: the East Asian NICs, Thailand, Malaysia, Turkey, Chile, and Mexico. At the end of this section, consideration is given as to how relationships with other countries, less far advanced in their economic policy changes, might adapt. As already noted, those countries have already abandoned policies of import substitution, removed virtually all quantitative restrictions, and greatly lowered their tariffs. Their difficulties in achieving deeper integration might be expected to be no greater than those of Spain and Portugal with accession to the EC.[11]

There are other instances of fairly deep integration between areas with very different per capita income levels. These include such diverse experiences as Hong Kong's laissez-faire regime during its rapid growth as one of the East Asian NICs, Puerto Rico's relationship with the United States, Italy's entry (and especially southern Italy's) into the European Community in the 1950s, Greece's subsequent accession, and then Spanish and Portuguese accession in the mid-1980s.[12]

Hong Kong's situation is well known. In this British colony, there were no barriers to trade and few interventions with economic activity that were subject to British commercial law. In that sense, Hong Kong was deeply integrated. As one of the Asian NICs, Hong Kong's economic growth occurred very quickly despite rapid immigration from the People's Republic of China and even before accelerated

---

Many analysts use "purchasing-power-parity" exchange rates to contrast income levels and on that basis, the relativities would be much smaller than those indicated here. However, official exchange rates seem the more relevant measure for estimating the impact of deeper integration since competition among tradable goods is at issue.

11. Turkey is scheduled to enter into customs union with the European Union on January 1, 1996.

12. Puerto Rico's experience might also be considered. Rapid economic growth and rising per capita incomes have accompanied integration with the U.S. economy. There are no trade barriers, and, by virtue of Commonwealth status, integration is deep: Puerto Rican economic activity takes place according to the same commercial code and regulations as govern activity on the mainland. (See Gregory and Reynolds [1965] for an analysis).

For purposes of examining the impact of deep integration on an area with a low per capita income, however, there are two special features of the Puerto Rican experience that make its usefulness dubious. First, labor flows between Puerto Rico and the U.S. mainland were unrestricted. Second, U.S. tax exemptions for Puerto Rico provided special incentives for locating production there.

Table 3-1. *Per Capita Income Differentials, 1980, 1991*[a]
Percent of weighted average of industrial countries' per capita income

Country	1980	1991
Italy	62.8	88.0
Portugal	23.0	28.2
Spain	52.3	59.1
Korea	14.7	30.1
Singapore	43.0	67.5
Thailand	6.5	7.5

Source: Author's calculations based on data from World Bank (1982, pp. 110–11); and World Bank (1993, pp. 238–39). Weighted average per capita income for the industrial countries is taken from "Industrial Market Economies" for 1980 and from "high-income OECD countries" for 1992.

a. Estimates at official exchange rates.

growth on the mainland provided further impetus for Hong Kong's growth. Although there is always room for debate about the factors that resulted in such rapid growth, clearly Hong Kong's laissez-faire regime was not inconsistent with growth.

When Italy signed the Treaty of Rome, its southern part was as poor, relative to Germany and France, as the advanced NICs are relative to the rich OECD countries of the 1990s. Although integration among EC countries in the early phases of the Community proceeded slowly, as late as 1980, Italian per capita income was estimated to be about two-thirds of the average for the rich OECD countries.

In many regards, however, the experience of Spain and Portugal in their accession to full membership in the European Communities invites attention.[13] Table 3-1 provides data on the per capita incomes of Spain, Portugal, and Italy relative to the rich OECD countries in 1980 and 1991, along with data for a few other developing countries. As late as 1980, Spain's per capita income is estimated to have been slightly more than half of that of the rich industrial countries as a group, while Italy's was around 63 percent. Portugal's was lower still, estimated at just less than a quarter of the rich industrial countries. By 1991, the latest year for which estimates are available, Korean per capita income relative to that of OECD countries exceeded that of Portugal in 1980, while Singapore's per capita income was relatively well above even the Italian numbers of a decade earlier.

13. I am indebted to Subitha Subramania at Duke University for valuable research assistance on Spain's accession to the EC.

Thus, for the most advanced of the middle-income developing countries, the lessons from Spanish, Portuguese, and Greek accession may be of some relevance. By and large, the lesson seems to be that countries with significantly different economic structures and at earlier stages of development can integrate with much less difficulty than most observers anticipated in the early 1980s. For simplicity, focus will be on Spain's accession, although the impact on Greece and Portugal does not seem to have been much different: negative impacts were far smaller than anticipated and growth accelerated in the years subsequent to entry.

Accession to the EC

Until the late 1950s, Spain was clearly a developing country, with policies not dissimilar to the import-substitution policies described in chapter 1. It was only after two stabilization programs in the late 1950s that Spain lowered its external trade barriers somewhat and began a fifteen-year period of very rapid economic growth.[14]

With the oil price increase of 1973, and the ensuing period of stagnation in Europe and other difficulties, Spain's economy stagnated. As late as 1983, the average tariff rate, inclusive of taxes levied only at the border, stood at 20 percent, with tariffs on some imports much higher. The tax-inclusive tariff rates on transport equipment and plastics, for example, were estimated to be more than 30 percent in that year. Tariffs on textiles, footwear and apparel, and nonmetallic mineral products also averaged higher than 20 percent.

Because Spain had retained so much protection against imports, it was widely anticipated that structural adjustment with EC entry would provide a significant shock. As stated by Hine, "In the short term, Spain and its EC partners have to come to terms with the adjustment problems created by Spain's membership of the EC customs union. These problems are particularly severe because Spain is both a large and heavily protected country, and a relatively poor one."[15]

Spain initially negotiated with the EC in the 1970s, after which time EC tariffs against Spanish products were substantially reduced,

14. See Sturc (1968) for an account of the economic situation in Spain prior to the stabilization programs and for a description of the programs.
15. Hine (1989, p. 1).

while Spain maintained its external protection and undertook to lower its tariffs upon accession at a later date. Thus the adjustment was expected to be asymmetrical, with Spanish adjustments greatly exceeding those of EC members.

It was thought that Spanish manufacturing was highly inefficient,[16] and that most industries would have a difficult time adjusting. Analysts pointed to the coexistence of many small, high-cost firms with large monopolistic producers, sheltered by tariffs and quotas from international competition. Iron and steel, nonferrous metals, and mechanicals were identified as sectors with structural problems. However, despite those concerns, the outcome of negotiations was to permit Spain seven years, instead of the normal five, for complete removal of all customs duties, quotas, and other forms of protection. Thus Spain had no border barriers against EU goods by January 1, 1993.[17]

The transition after accession seems to have gone much more smoothly than the fears voiced at the time of negotiations for entry implied. Spain (and Portugal) experienced far more rapid growth in the five years after entry than they had in earlier years. Real investment rose sharply. The OECD commented:

> The strong upturn in activity, which started in late 1985, continued unabated up to the middle of 1989. During this period the economy grew by more than 5 percent per annum, leading to a marked fall in unemployment from a peak rate of 22 percent in 1985 to just over 16.5 percent in mid-1989. While the strength and profile of the upswing statistically mirrors in large measure the extent and long duration of the preceding downturn of the economy, the vigour of the expansionary phase cannot be explained

16. Problems for agricultural adjustment were quite different. Spain had to become a full member of the Common Agricultural Policy and the main questions were about Spanish competition with other Mediterranean countries. It was estimated that immediate application of EC support prices to Spain would have increased Spanish agricultural income by 14 percent. Although some components of agriculture (such as dairy products) would face adjustment problems in Spain, the major motives for slowing the transition stemmed from anticipated European problems of adjustment, not Spanish. For that reason, they are not further dealt with here. It should be noted, however, that the negotiated solution normally focused on the length of the transition period rather than on enduring "special arrangements."

17. For a discussion of the prospective problems of Spanish manufacturing, see Donges and Schatz (1989, p. 267). The Spanish iron and steel industry, and the textile and clothing industry, were given additional support for restructuring, but quotas were retained on exports to other EC countries for the transition period. See Hine (1989) for a discussion.

without reference to the structural reforms undertaken in the first half of the 1980s and the positive effects of EC entry since 1986.[18]

By 1991, some analysts pointed to the Spanish market as being the second most rapidly growing in the world.[19]

In OECD reports and other commentaries, one can now find little mention of integration with the EC as a source of difficulty. By any measure, one must conclude that Spanish accession proceeded with much greater benefits and fewer adjustment costs than were anticipated by many.[20]

Some observers have noted that large transfers from richer EC countries to poorer members may buffer the transition in ways not available to developing countries if they pursue deeper integration with developed countries. However, in Spain's case transfers from the EC were short-lived. By 1992, it was estimated that all transfers from the EC amounted to less than 0.5 percent of Spanish GDP, while the costs to Spanish industry of meeting EU environmental standards was anticipated to be $12 billion over the subsequent five years.[21]

Portugal, as seen in table 3-1, was and is much poorer than Spain, and economic growth, although accelerating in the years following the start of transition, was not as rapid as in Spain. There is little evidence, however, that Portugal's economy was subject to more difficulties than it would have been in the absence of EC entry. Indeed, there is at least as much reason for believing that Portugal might be even worse off had it remained outside the EC.

The arrangements for Spanish and Portuguese entry into the EC provided for a transitional period during which adjustments could occur. But during that period, fairly complete deep integration took place. Measures included tax alignments, adoption of EC banking standards and regulations, and, more recently, efforts to meet the Maastricht targets.

Both countries had external trade barriers at least as high, if not higher, than do the very advanced NICs in the mid-1990s. Their

18. OECD (1991, p. 11).

19. Christopher Lynch, "Spain 1992 and Beyond," *Business America*, August 26, 1991, p. 2.

20. Spain entered into recession in 1992 along with other EU countries. For Spain, the problems of monetary union appeared to be especially daunting in view of the higher-than-EC-average Spanish rate of inflation and continuing difficulties in achieving the fiscal targets set under Maastricht, which call for inflation not more than 2 percent above the average for all members.

21. "After the Fiesta: A Survey of Spain," *Economist*, April 25, 1992, p. 6.

income levels, relative to the rich EC countries, were not much different from those of Korea, Taiwan, and Singapore relative to the rich OECD countries today.

Mexican Entry into NAFTA

Mexican accession to NAFTA illustrates several points.[22] First, the Mexican authorities did try to alter many of their domestic regulations and to accept elements of common standards. Although some of these arrangements were conducive to Mexico's economic objectives, others were clearly accepted as the price to be paid for deeper integration with Canada and the United States.[23]

Second, there appears, at least to date, to have been very little opposition to joining NAFTA in Mexico: indeed, by and large, it seems to have been a popular move.[24] Opposition was far more intense in the United States, which suggests that it may be resistance in developed countries, rather than difficulties in developing countries, which will provide the real constraint to deeper integration between developed and developing countries.

Third, one of the benefits the Mexicans wanted to achieve through accession to NAFTA was an increased flow of private foreign investment, especially direct foreign investment. It was reasoned that, with the assurances of NAFTA that Mexican policies would remain stable, foreign investors would be willing to invest in more and larger projects in Mexico than would otherwise have been the case.

Fourth, Mexico's motives for accession to NAFTA seem to have involved not only the benefits of increased access to the large North American market, but also the locking in of policy reforms under-

22. This section was written in the fall of 1994, before the financial crisis that engulfed Mexico, starting with the 15 percent devaluation in December 1994, occurred. Although it is too early to provide a definitive assessment of the factors contributing to the crisis, two points are evident: Mexican exchange rate policy had identifiably been a major weak point in the reform program and had been maintained despite the East German example of what can go wrong at an inappropriate exchange rate; and the political difficulties of 1994 clearly contributed to the outcome. There is a reasonable basis for believing, therefore, that the crisis would have occurred in the absence of NAFTA, although the fact that the Mexican economy was more open undoubtedly intensified the crisis.

23. For the particulars of the NAFTA agreement see Hufbauer and Schott (1992).

24. To be sure, the Chiapas uprising in January 1994 was timed to start with accession to NAFTA but appears to have centered on social issues pertaining to the indigenous population rather than on NAFTA accession.

taken in Mexico. Mexico had already removed almost all quantitative restrictions and had lowered tariffs to an average height of around 10 percent. On trade account, the Mexican authorities had already undertaken measures to open their economy. The ability to commit to NAFTA was seen by the Mexican authorities as an added element of credibility indicating that the altered Mexican regime would be permanent. Since achieving credibility after policy reforms is often one of the key challenges, this in itself was important for Mexico.[25]

The benefits the Mexicans hoped to achieve from NAFTA did not come without concessions on their part. They included the side agreements on labor and the environment, as well as acceptance of phytosanitary standards and several other provisions that were arguably costly to the Mexican economy, at least in the short run. In Mexico, clearly, officials judged that whatever costs these measures of deeper integration would impose were well worthwhile in light of the expected benefits.

The rapidity with which the Mexican economy went from an import-substitution-oriented, quantitative-restrictions import regime as late as 1985 to an outer-oriented economy set to join NAFTA surprised many analysts. Within the NAFTA agreement, most of the measures agreed on are according to a timetable so that changes are set to take place over a period up to ten years and sometimes even fifteen.

Mexico's changes in policies and accession to NAFTA dramatically illustrate the speed with which developing countries can alter their trade and payments regimes, undertake policy reforms, and be in a position to accept measures for deeper integration. There is no doubt that considerable opening of the trade regime, moves toward a sustainable exchange rate policy, greater currency convertibility, and removal of other state controls are prerequisites for entry into deeper integration arrangements. Even once those policy reforms are undertaken, countries in a position to consider deeper integration will be able to implement agreements over periods of a decade and longer, just as Mexico, Spain, and others have done. If negotiations can permit an adequate time for meeting standards of deeper integration, the experience of Mexico, Spain, and Portugal (along with that of

25. That integration cannot substitute for sustainable policies is, however, demonstrated by the subsequent difficulties with exchange rate and financial management.

Hong Kong, Puerto Rico, and others) would suggest that, once advanced NIC status is attained, participation in deeper integration can on net provide a further stimulus for growth and not produce intolerable strains on the economies of those countries. However, it seems clear that having an appropriate policy framework prior to integration is essential.

Deeper Integration and Threats to Developing Countries

The ease with which Spain, Portugal, Mexico, and others have joined arrangements for deeper integration has surprised observers. So, too, however, did the strength of the opposition to NAFTA that was aroused in the United States. Whereas prior to the NAFTA debate in the United States, analysts had been inclined to question the willingness and ability of developing countries to enter into integration arrangements, the experience of the NAFTA debate and subsequent events have aroused concerns that developed countries will not accept deeper integration with developing countries, or at least will not accept deeper integration on terms that enable developing countries to achieve their developmental objectives.

It has already been seen that, despite the delays and disputes that prolonged negotiations, the Uruguay Round agreement represented great progress in extending the scope of GATT disciplines and strengthening the multilateral trading system. It also represented a breakthrough in developing countries' relationships to GATT.

For the first time, the developing countries recognized the reality of the interdependence of their fortunes with the health of the world economy. The developing countries were full partners in the round, bargaining for their interests—especially on agriculture, textiles, and apparel—and conceding on issues (such as intellectual property rights) deemed important by the developed countries.

For the most part, the concessions by each group of countries were really actions in their own self-interest. Nonetheless, in the parlance of multilateral trade negotiations, the final agreement represented a compromise between developed and developing countries. The developed countries achieved agreement from the developing countries to "tariffy" most of their quantitative restrictions, to reduce tariffs and barriers to agricultural imports, to adopt the measures necessary to ensure certain levels of intellectual property rights, and to remove various conditions on investment.[26] In turn, the developing countries achieved agreements to bring the Multifiber Arrangement under GATT discipline, to liberalize agricultural trade, and to modify several other trade measures about which they were concerned.[27]

Imagine, then, the surprise with which developing countries' leaders and trade officials heard the announcement in April 1994 from the Clinton administration and the French that the agreement would not be signed at Marrakesh unless it were understood that consideration would be given to the adoption of labor standards early in the existence of the new World Trade Organization (WTO). Because the comparative advantage of many of the developing countries lies so heavily in products intensive in the use of unskilled labor, concern naturally arises about any proposals for labor standards.[28]

Unlike measures such as enforcement of intellectual property rights, which has at least a possible rationale grounded in economic efficiency, the case for labor standards cannot be made in terms of economic efficiency nor even in terms of the impact on the poor in the developing countries.[29] Indeed, the imposition of labor standards across countries to

26. Of these agreements, the only one that was arguably *not* in developing countries' self-interest was intellectual property rights. Even in that instance, there are potential identifiable gains, as well as losses. The more advanced developing countries will, in hindsight, have probably gained by adopting protection for IPRs. For the less advanced countries the losses incurred by paying royalties, licensing and copyright fees, and otherwise abiding by the new code may in the short run outweigh the direct benefits of intellectual property protection. For an analysis, see Deardorff (1992) and Chin and Grossman (1990).

27. For example, developing countries have long opposed selectivity in safeguards, by which is meant the ability of a (presumably developed) country to use its GATT-sanctioned escape clause legislation against an individual exporting country. The fear is that any such selectivity could be used to discriminate against developing countries.

28. See also Ehrenberg (1994) in this series. Ehrenberg analyzes many of the same aspects of labor standards as this volume does, primarily from the perspective of developed countries, and he shows the difficulties that would be involved for deeper integration even then. For developing countries at an early stage of development, all of Ehrenberg's arguments apply in force in addition to the considerations raised here.

29. This is not to say that the developing countries may not lose from stricter enforcement of intellectual property rights. Indeed, it has been estimated that losses on pharmaceuticals for some countries may be as high as 700 percent. (See Rodrik [1994, p. 16]). However, the case for intellectual property rights protection rests on the proposition that, unless developers of new products or techniques are permitted to earn a return on those techniques, the flow of new innovations will dry up. In that sense, protection of intellectual property everywhere represents a trade-off between today (where the principle that static

the extent they increase labor costs in poor countries is as protectionist from the viewpoint of rich countries as is the imposition of tariffs on labor-intensive goods.

Many of the objections were to "competing with cheap labor" or to competing with firms where environmental standards are "not as high as in developed countries." Although superficially these arguments appear plausible, on closer inspection they are problematic. Sorting out legitimate concerns from protectionist pressures masked under calls for labor, environmental, or other standards is a great challenge.

The importance of trade and access to developed countries' markets for developing countries has already been seen. The advantages of trade to developing countries are precisely that they can export goods and services that use the factors that these countries have in abundance. In return, they can import other goods and services that are more intensive in the use of factors that are scarce for them and relatively more abundant in the developed countries: goods with high research and development content and goods that use relatively large amounts of skilled labor and capital.

If deeper integration is undertaken only with accompanying measures that prevent developing countries from using their comparative advantage, deeper integration could pose a significant threat to the prospects for economic growth and rising living standards in poor countries.[30] Requiring poor countries to enforce uneconomically high labor and environmental standards would in effect be robbing them of part or all of their comparative advantage. Raising tariffs on imports of goods intensive in the use of unskilled labor could, for example, have protectionist effects equivalent to requiring high labor standards. If failure to conform to those standards were then used as a reason for denying developing countries access to markets, the

---

economic well-being can be maximized by pricing all goods at marginal cost applies) and the future (where a margin above marginal cost will enable firms to recover research, development, and start-up costs). Developing countries may lose somewhat from higher prices of proprietary goods in the present, but they gain prospectively by the provision of more such goods in the future.

30. When the announcement concerning labor standards prior to Marrakesh was made by the United States, many developing countries objected. The most vocal was, naturally, India. See, for example, Stefan Wagstyl, "India Warns over Labor Controls," *Financial Times*, May 6, 1994, p. 5, where India's commerce minister said that these proposals were tantamount "to introducing protectionism through the back door." The *Financial Times* reported in the same article that the insistence on labor standards had increased the political difficulties faced by the leaders of economic policy reform in India.

effects of such actions would be extremely detrimental to growth prospects for developing countries.

It is therefore necessary to evaluate pleas for labor and environmental standards carefully. For it is on the treatment of these issues in plans for deeper integration that the fate of the developing countries is likely to hang.

A first question is what labor standards are or might be. There are three separate issues involved. Some proposals center on a minimum global wage, which, if high enough to be above the wage prevailing in poor developing countries, would clearly impinge on the ability of poor countries to rely on an outer-oriented trade strategy for development. A second group of proposals focuses on minimum safety standards, conditions of employment, maximal hours of work, and so on. To a great degree, these proposals, too, would increase the cost of employing labor in developing countries and thus reduce the comparative advantage of labor-abundant countries. The third and final group of proposals concerns the employment of child and prison labor.

Even the third group of proposals can be viewed as protectionist and could be expected to raise the cost of employing labor, but it also raises other issues pertaining to the functioning of labor markets.

Developing countries have low incomes because productivity is low. Low productivity has several causes. Many workers in developing countries have few, if any, skills that contribute to higher productivity; many workers also lack experience. A large fraction of the work force in some poor developing countries is illiterate and probably cannot be productively employed in urban jobs. Moreover, capital per worker, in individual lines of economic activity and in infrastructure, is low. With real rates of return on capital high and unskilled labor relatively abundant and cheap, firms have an incentive to use labor-intensive methods when possible.[31] That in turn results in lower labor productivity (but, of course, more employment).[32]

31. Even when production methods themselves do not permit a great deal of substitution of capital for labor, many "supporting" operations, such as packaging of products and materials handling, can be accomplished with labor-using or capital-using techniques. Hence, substitution of labor for capital usually takes place in some aspects of factory operations even in firms that are engaged in production techniques that require additional capital. See the individual country studies in Krueger and others (1981).

32. The average hourly manufacturing wage in Germany was $14.42 in 1993, while that in the United States was $11.74. Would the Germans be justified in insisting on an American minimum wage close to their level? Author's calculations based on ILO (1994).

For a country abundant with unskilled labor, the early years of an outer-oriented trade strategy will be years in which entrepreneurs produce goods competitively by combining cheap unskilled labor with other scarcer, and more expensive, factors in labor-intensive processes. Anything that raises costs will reduce competitiveness and hence the rate at which learning, investment, and other factors can raise productivity and thus permit increases in wages without undermining competitiveness.

As policy reforms are undertaken and labor-abundant developing countries switch to an outer-oriented trade strategy, the initial situation in the labor market is usually one in which relatively high minimum wage legislation, taxes on labor, union power, or other regulations governing employment of factory workers have resulted in a "dual" labor market. One of the challenges of policy reform is to alter this situation so that reliance can be placed on comparative advantage for the establishment and growth of nontraditional exports.

In a dual labor market, high wages for those with jobs (enforced by government regulations or by union power) generally result in a formal sector of the economy where wages and working conditions are very good compared with those in the rest of the economy. However, the number of persons employed in the formal sector is limited. This sector usually includes the government, large capital-intensive firms, and other large-scale economic activities where the high visibility of the firms' activities makes breaches of the legal wage standard or of union rights costly for them.[33]

Coexisting with the formal sector is normally an informal sector where wages are much lower and where working conditions and fringe benefits are far less generous than in the formal sector.[34] As a

33. The formal sector is normally seen to include those firms dependent on government privileges such as protection from imports and access to credit at subsidized interest rates. It is generally thought that most exporting needs to be undertaken by firms whose size is large enough to make them visible because the need to produce appropriate documents for exports and to develop marketing, quality control, and other capabilities normally dictates a scale of activity that is large by standards of developing countries.

34. For one estimate for a variety of countries of the wage differentials and their effects, see the studies in Krueger and others (1981). There are many good theoretical analyses of the impact of high wages in the formal sector. See, for example, Bhagwati and Srinivasan (1974) for an analysis of the effects on trade, Fields (1994) for an analysis incorporating the informal sector, and Harris and Todaro (1970) for the original analyses when there is open unemployment.

consequence, capital and productivity per worker are usually vastly lower in the informal sector than in the formal sector. In countries where these conditions occur, often significant numbers of people are seeking work in the formal sector. In some instances, they are unemployed; in other instances, they are engaged in low-productivity occupations that permit them to spend part of their time seeking work in the formal sector of the economy.

Raising the wage in the formal sector of the economy normally reduces future employment in the formal sector for several reasons.[35] First, employers must achieve higher levels of labor productivity to maintain profitability at its existing level (which usually means employing more capital-using methods, which requires additional investment). Insofar as additional investment is aimed at achieving that higher productivity, it cannot be aimed at expanding job opportunities at existing capital-labor ratios. Second, labor-intensive activities in the formal sector become higher cost and are thus less likely to expand output or to develop and expand new export markets. Third, at a higher wage rate, investments will normally be made with more capital-using processes, at least in the peripheral activities already mentioned. Thus fewer new employment opportunities for any given level of aggregate savings and investment will occur.[36]

All three of these mechanisms seem to operate in countries where efforts have been made to enforce a wage in the formal sector much above what would prevail if labor markets were permitted to function. Remember that anything that raises unit labor costs to firms has the same effect as an increase in the wage. Thus increased payroll taxes, requirements that firms build schools for the education of their workers, and high social insurance payments can all contribute to

35. When the wage rate rises, employment will generally be less extensive than at a lower wage. But when the wage rate rises *because* productivity has increased and there is excess demand for labor, that is a sign of healthy economic growth. The discussion in the text assumes an "exogenous" upward shift, perhaps because of a large increase in the legislated minimum wage, that is, in the wage to be paid in the formal sector of the economy when many would be willing and able to work in that sector at the existing wage.

36. If government controls enforce the allocation of credit to "formal sector" enterprises, it is of course possible that a higher fraction of available resources will be allocated to the formal sector. If that happens, then the available capital per worker in the informal sector will fall, and the result will be an even larger differential in the wage between the formal and the informal sector.

driving a wedge between conditions of employment in the formal and informal sectors.[37]

Very often, therefore, when policy reform efforts begin, regulations surrounding the functioning of labor markets must be changed if policy reform is to be successful in permitting a shift to an outer-oriented trade strategy and more rapid economic growth. When labor markets are reformed, any reductions in the wage rate in the formal sector necessarily disadvantage those already employed in the formal sector, but they permit the expansion of employment for the truly poor—those who were previously unemployed or employed at much lower wages in the informal sector.

Korea illustrates this proposition. In order for employers to find it economically viable to hire unskilled workers in labor-intensive industries, a reasonably low wage is necessary in the early stages of development. In the late 1950s, before the start of Korean reforms, the "formal sector" wage in Korea's import-substitution sector was far above the rural wage, where more than 70 percent of the population was employed. Estimates show that the formal sector urban wage was more than three times the rural wage. Simultaneously, however, unemployment, estimated at 25 percent of the urban labor force, was very high.[38]

Thus in the 1950s, Korea had a dual labor market, with high wages for those working in the formal urban (import-substitution) industries, but at the expense of fewer jobs in those sectors and lower wages in the informal and rural parts of the economy. For the first four years after reforms were under way, real wages in the urban sector fell, but employment rose dramatically (table 3-2).

As can be seen in table 3-2, nonagricultural employment was falling until 1960, although the real wage was increasing through 1959 (as mandated by law). One of the 1960s reforms was to liberal-

37. There is some evidence that legislation protecting workers' jobs can have similar effects. When reforms were under way in Chile, several of them effectively reduced the differential between formal and informal sector labor costs. It has been estimated that the reform that had the most effect in terms of increasing the demand for labor was the removal of a regulation that, in effect, gave workers the right to life-long employment after they had been employed for a year. In order to avoid the liability and inflexibility of a large permanent labor force, Chilean employers had resorted to more capital-using methods than they did once they achieved greater flexibility in employing their workers. See, for example, Corbo and de Melo (1987).

38. Kim and Roemer (1979).

Table 3-2. *Korean Wages and Urban Employment during Years of Rapid Growth*

Year	Off-farm employment (000)	Real wages (1970 = 100)	Year	Off-farm employment (000)	Real wages (1970 = 100)
1957	2,010	54.8	1976	6,700	151.8
1958	1,950	61.3	1977	7,280	175.8
1959	1,940	62.5	1978	7,950	206.3
1960	2,150	57.3	1979	8,310	226.4
1961	2,550	60.5	1980	8,590	213.3
1962	2,580	60.8	1981	8,890	206.0
1963	2,720	57.9	1982	9,610	225.6
1964	2,810	54.9	1983	10,200	245.1
1965	3,140	56.8	1984	10,510	259.1
1966	3,300	59.0	1985	11,237	276.4
1967	3,650	65.5	1986	11,843	291.1
1968	4,000	72.8	1987	12,274	311.0
1969	4,260	89.7	1988	13,386	335.3
1970	4,630	100.0	1989	14,093	383.9
1971	5,050	109.2	1990	14,744	420.2
1972	5,220	111.4	1991	15,473	450.5
1973	5,510	119.5	1992	15,896	487.9
1974	5,880	133.9			
1975	6,230	113.5			

Sources: Author's calculations based on data from ILO (1993); IMF (1993); Krueger (1987, p. 197). Nominal wage data from ILO were deflated by IMF price data.

ize the labor market. Initially, the result was a decrease in the real wage. However, employment in the urban sector (where the wage was above the level in rural areas) began growing rapidly, and the unemployment rate began falling dramatically from its 1960 level recorded as 25 percent of the urban labor force. By 1973, real wages were virtually double their 1960 level, while nonagricultural employment had almost tripled. During this period, Korea's production and exports of unskilled labor-intensive goods were increasing rapidly.

Thereafter, urban wages rose rapidly but without any duality in the labor market. To be sure, older people in rural areas (many of them had very low levels of literacy and no industrial work experience) had bleaker economic fortunes than those urban workers who were gaining experience, but nevertheless the real wage began rising rapidly and employment grew very quickly.

As rapid growth continued, fewer farm workers were available to enter the nonagricultural labor force, and real wages began rising even more rapidly. In consequence, Korea's comparative advantage in goods obtained by using relatively large amounts of unskilled labor began to diminish. By the early 1990s, Korean real wages are estimated to have been about seven times their level in the late 1950s, and urban employment was seven times its earlier level.[39]

Korean law protecting unions' rights was very weak during this growth and was strengthened greatly after 1987. Interestingly, Gary L. Fields finds no evidence that strengthening affected real wages: they rose at about the same rate as productivity and do not appear to have been repressed prior to changes in labor law.[40]

Clearly, by the early 1990s, Korea could no longer expect to be competitive in labor-intensive goods (nor would it have been economic to produce and export them). But in the 1960s had Korea been subject to a high real minimum wage or labor standards that raised labor costs commensurately, it is evident that, at a minimum, growth of production and exports would have been slower and might not have taken place at all.

Labor Standards?

What, then, are the arguments for labor standards? As already seen, three separate sets of ideas predominate. The first is the notion that wages are "too low" and therefore represent "unfair" competition. Other arguments profess concern with workers' well-being and assert that although wage differentials are acceptable, health, safety, and other conditions of employment should be agreed upon and minimum standards set. The third set of concerns has focused on labor practices that are found predominantly, if not exclusively, in developing countries: child labor is the dominant issue.

It is evident that setting a global minimum wage at a level above that prevailing in the poorest countries would deprive those countries of much of their comparative advantage. If, for example, a

39. See the analysis in Fields (1994) for a survey of the evidence regarding labor markets in the newly industrialized economies. Fields notes that real wages grew rapidly, at an average rate slightly above the rate of growth of labor productivity and concludes that "repression" could not have been an issue.

40. Fields (1994).

deep-integration scheme were implemented under which the minimum global wage were double that prevailing in India, India's exporters would clearly be disadvantaged relative to their competitors in countries where the agreed-upon minimum was just above that negotiated and where labor productivity was much higher.

Some have argued that wages are so low in some developing countries that their level is clear evidence that wages are kept "artificially low" and that there is "exploitation" of workers and that therefore raising wages would only reduce profits and would not affect output or employment. If those charges were generally correct, evidence of excess demand for labor in developing countries would appear. In fact, even in countries such as Korea with rising real wages and rapidly growing nonfarm employment, there seems to be an excess supply of workers seeking employment. Although pockets of exploitation may occur, any increases in wages that workers would receive as a result of global minimum wages would have to be weighed against the losses incurred by lower levels of nonfarm employment (and hence wages) for other workers who failed to find jobs as a result of the global wage. Those workers would probably be employed (producing nontradables) at wages below the agreed-upon standard. The net effect would be to reduce exports, growth prospects, and living standards, *and* to reduce wages for workers in the nontradable informal sector.

Although safety standards are a concern to all, it must be recognized that improving industrial safety is also not a costless activity. Just as raising the global minimum wage would adversely affect employment, so too would raising labor costs by imposing the standards of the rich countries on the poor. In an important sense, standards have to be set relative to each country's overall economic performance and level of labor productivity. To insist that, for example, Bangladeshi employers adhere to the same safety standards as German employers would be to raise the costs of employment and hence reduce prospects for other, even poorer, members of the labor force.

Perhaps the most troublesome issue, however, is that of standards regarding prison and child labor. Prison labor is already outlawed under GATT and ILO conventions and therefore need not be of concern here.

Everyone of any sensibility in rich countries naturally abhors the employment of children for long hours in conditions that are intolerable by the standards of developed countries. It is tempting and almost instinctive to conclude that the solution must be to ban the importation of goods produced with the use of child labor.

But in the poverty prevailing in developing countries, what are the likely effects of such a ban? No parent can possibly want a child to be working. But given conditions of poverty in many developing countries, serious questions arise about what would happen if such labor were outlawed. For some families, children's earnings—which seem pitifully small by rich countries' standards—may make a significant difference to the family's budget. In some instances, children (especially girls) may be enabled to stay at home and to avoid alternatives (which for girls may be early marriages) that are seen as worse than factory employment.

Although possibly some children employed long hours in factories might otherwise be sent to school, that seems less likely than the occurrence of less pleasant alternatives, such as begging. Considerable evidence shows that, as per capita incomes rise, parents voluntarily enroll their children in school.[41] In countries where primary schooling is far from universal, questions about the allocation of scarce educational resources also arise.

These considerations provide the overriding reason for being extremely cautious about imposing global standards. A practical question also arises: if standards were imposed, should there be a ban on child labor applying to all goods produced in the country when child labor is used anywhere, or should a ban apply only to importation of goods directly dependent on child labor? And, if the former, what of child labor in agriculture, where children are almost universally employed at harvest time? Enforcement would prove exceptionally difficult, and one wonders whether it could possibly prevail in countries such as China.

On close inspection, it seems reasonable to conclude that support for labor standards comes from many well-meaning individuals who cannot imagine the depth of poverty in developing countries and from those representing protectionist interests in the developed countries.[42]

41. "Workers of the World, Compete," *Economist,* April 2, 1994, p. 73; and Martin Wolf, "Protectionist Standards," *Financial Times,* July 4, 1994, p. 20.

42. There is an issue that arises on occasion. Children have been employed in some activities, such as making glass bangles, where conditions are extremely damaging to health. Any international efforts to mandate safety standards, however, would have to balance the

Although there may be some benefits arising from elimination of pockets of exploitation and employers' monopsony power, any such benefits would have to be weighed against the costs of reducing or eliminating the benefits of an open trading policy for other labor-abundant countries.

Environmental Concerns

Just as the issue of labor standards has been seized upon by those wanting protection for other reasons, calls for trade measures in relation to environmental issues must be carefully assessed to determine whether proposals, whose appeal is based on environmental concerns, may not be protectionist in intent.[43]

Moreover, just as some of the well-intentioned advocacy for labor standards arises from a misunderstanding of the causes of low wages and poor working conditions and of the probable economic consequences of such measures, some of the legitimate concern for the environment could also lead to advocacy of trade-related policies that would result in environmental deterioration rather than improvement.

However, whereas most calls for labor standards are based on the false premise that resources really are there and that wages can be increased with few adverse effects on the number employed, there is no question but that there are some very real environmental concerns. The question is whether those concerns can be addressed at all effectively through trade measures. Moreover, some of the key issues come to the fore between developed and developing countries.

There is another significant difference between the advocacy of labor standards and environmental protection. Few would argue that low wages for workers with low labor productivity in developing countries have spillover effects. But many recognize that there are

---

benefits from improvement in some circumstances from the costs where in fact protectionist interests are being served. There are also, for reasons discussed above related to administrative capacity, concerns about poor countries' ability to enforce such standards.

43. Much of the argument in this section is based on the proposition that trade is an inappropriate instrument to use to seek accords with developing countries on practices that have negative global environmental impacts. Accords on the environment itself will be necessary. See Cooper (1994) in this series for an in-depth discussion.

environmental spillovers. The difficult questions surround the link between the environment and trade issues.

Several phenomena must be considered. The history of environmental concerns in the now-rich countries, how people at different income levels react to their environment, and the range of environmental spillovers will clearly affect the possibility of achieving rational policies or intentional accords.

The now-rich countries despoiled their environments in the nineteenth century in the process of economic growth. Life expectancies were low, and other more pressing concerns occupied people at low levels of income. In part, producing greater productive capacity enabled environmental cleanup to take place at a later date.

Either way, people in developing countries are poor. They do not choose to expend the same resources as do citizens in developed countries, not because they want a polluted environment, but because of their budget constraints. Moreover, they are fully cognizant that the inhabitants of rich countries devastated their own environments a century ago. Efforts to impose environmental restraints and standards on developing countries at early stages of development can be viewed as the rich countries' efforts to keep the wealth for themselves.

Moreover, the available evidence suggests that environmental degradation occurs at low per capita incomes, rising until per capita income reaches around $5,000 (at prices of around 1990). Thereafter, pollution tends to be reduced as incomes rise further.[44] Since it may be taken for granted that developing countries will not abandon their growth and developmental objectives and accept permanently low per capita incomes for their citizens, anything that reduces the rate at which they reach their objective could increase total pollution. Should a trade weapon be used in pursuit of environmental objectives, it could clearly have that effect, given the importance of the international economy for growth prospects in developing countries. Thus if trade sanctions were imposed against developing countries that failed to meet costly environmental standards, that could prove counterproductive even for those with environmental concerns. Alternatively, if developing countries accepted the costs of those standards in order to maintain market access and consequently reduced other investments

44. See Grossman and Krueger (1991).

(to finance the necessary expenditures to meet the standards) in ways that slowed down their growth, any short-run benefits to the environment could be offset by later effects. This would happen if there were a longer time period during which pollution was increasing before per capita incomes reached a level at which people chose to reduce them.[45]

Environmental concerns fall into two groups: one in which there are global, or at least multicountry, externalities from the polluting activity in a given place; and the other in which all negative externalities are in the country where the pollution takes place. For the latter case, there is little reason for international concern. Indeed, it can be argued that preferences within the country determine how much other consumption to sacrifice for a cleaner environment (just as in developed countries). Moreover, in poor countries where pressing day-to-day consumption needs lead to few expenditures on environmental issues, it can be argued that the lower costs of pollution there in contrast to costs to rich countries can and should legitimately be a part of those countries' comparative advantage.[46] If people in rich countries are willing to pay large sums for environmental cleanup, or for use of nonpolluting techniques of production, whereas people in poor countries do not choose to do so, people in both countries are better off with trade. In the poor country, incomes are higher, and in the rich country environmental objectives are reached at lower cost. To impose high clean-up costs on people in poor countries certainly would reduce their comparative advantage in some activities, just as would the imposition of labor standards higher than those that can yield relatively full employment in poor countries.

This point leads, however, to consideration of environmental issues characterized by global, or multicountry, externalities. In those cases, it seems clear that a multilateral accord is the appropriate path to take and that trade sanctions are an inappropriate mechanism for achieving desired goals. On one hand, it is difficult to enforce trade sanc-

45. Because of the perception in developing countries that the rich have already plundered their own environments, a serious risk arises that efforts to impose environmental standards will result in a backlash and induce citizens in developing countries to fail to take steps they would otherwise have taken when their resources do increase.

46. The developing countries are resentful when the developed countries attempt to impose their environmental standards.

tions beyond the point of refusing imports produced with pollutants. Yet production of nontraded goods and import-competing goods may be as intensive, if not more intensive, in the use of polluting materials or activities than the exportables in question. On the other hand, it would be politically difficult—if not infeasible and inappropriate on other grounds—to cut off all trade for those countries failing to adhere to environmental standards decreed by developed countries.

When externalities do exist, the real issue pertaining to global environmental concerns the allocation of pollutant rights. The conflict between developed and developing countries is a real one. Developed countries naturally want to see the allocation of such rights in rough proportion to pollutant levels (so that presumably the pain of cutback or reduced increase is relatively equally shared). Developing countries believe that pollutant rights should be granted in proportion to population, on the grounds that their incomes will increase and potential utilization should be the appropriate criterion.[47]

That issue cannot, and should not, be determined by or linked to trade policy. Aside from the risks already mentioned that such linkages will prove counterproductive, international accords seem preferable and are perhaps the only way to achieve enforcement in poorer countries.

Some environmentalists have argued that the existence of foreign competition makes resistance to desired environmental standards greater than it would otherwise be. The answer to that assertion depends on the possibility of multicountry spillovers. First, with appropriate international agreements when there are spillovers, each country can determine the mechanisms best suited to meet its commitments. In most instances, those mechanisms will raise costs for domestic users of the offending materials or producers of the undesirable waste. With appropriate mechanisms for resale of pollutant rights in each country, the resultant pricing of pollution rights should ensure that those countries that have lower costs are not "competing un-

---

47. It has been suggested that, if rich countries are keen to achieve a more rapid rate of improvement of the environment than developing countries believe that they can afford, perhaps rich countries could finance part or all of the expenditures of the developing countries.

fairly." For pollutants that are only local, the argument given above applies: if another country has less preference for a clean environment, because of different tastes or because incomes are lower, that can be a part of comparative advantage and should not be interfered with.[48]

48. It is also often noted that, at least to date, the magnitude of cost increases resulting from environmental standards in rich countries has seldom exceeded 3 percent to 4 percent. As such, one must question the extent to which the issue is real and the extent to which protection-seekers are simply reaching for a convenient argument.

Chapter 4

Conclusion

*T*HE DEVELOPING countries are opening their economies. Some have done so and are well on their way to advanced country status. Others are in process and beginning to witness increasing openness and a larger share of trade in GDP. Still others have yet to begin the process of reversing their former, largely ineffectual, import-substitution stance.

The rapidity with which each of these groups of countries can participate fully in deeper integration naturally varies. Policy reforms, including removal of quantitative restrictions and high tariffs on imports, and changes to a realistic exchange rate and more balanced incentives for exporting, clearly must come first. Failure to have achieved these essential changes can result in severe short-term hardships and even induce a reversal of policies in the longer run.

However, as the experience of Spain, Portugal, and other countries shows, after reforms have been in process for a reasonable time, moves toward deeper integration on a phased-in timetable are feasible. Already, agreement has been reached on many measures under the Uruguay Round agreement. Some measures are in the individual countries' self-interest, for example, tariff reductions and the liberalization of services trade. Other measures, however, such as the treatment of intellectual property rights, may entail short-run costs, and the developing countries agreed to them in return for improved access to markets for their products.

As further liberalization of trade in services and other aspects of deeper integration are considered by developed countries, developing countries will be examining how much those measures are truly designed to enhance the functioning of the global economy, as contrasted with the extent they may deprive developing countries of their comparative advantage. Most measures of the former type can constitute items for action for those developing countries that have already opened their economies. Perhaps they may need a somewhat longer timetable to implement them than that granted to developed countries.

Measures that in effect impose very high costs on developing countries or serve protectionist ends of special interests in developed countries are, however, a different matter. The two issues most discussed after Marrakesh have been labor and environmental standards. Imposition of labor standards could have effects very similar to the imposition by industrialized countries of high tariff barriers against imports from low-income countries and could wipe out much of the potential gain from policy reform, an open trade regime, and deeper integration. Should that happen, prospects for economic growth in those countries would be seriously jeopardized, and leaders in poor developing countries would question whether they should then accede to measures, such as intellectual property rights, in which the developed countries have a strong interest.

Use of trade sanctions, or threats of sanctions, to enforce environmental goals could have equally troublesome effects, especially when the environmental measures sought are costly and do not have spillovers from one country to another. The response to most proposals for labor standards must be to make the point that their imposition has the effect of raising labor costs and therefore reducing developing countries' comparative advantages in unskilled labor-intensive goods. Demands for environmental action, however, should be met by a proposal to seek international accords on issues in which there are multicountry effects.

Although environmental issues are important, so is the global trading system. To saddle that system with mechanisms for carrying out environmental regulation is not only likely to be destructive of the trading system, it is unlikely to achieve the desired environmental purposes.

If environmental issues can be handled under international agreements, while trade relations are under the aegis of a strengthened multilateral trading system under the World Trade Organization, prospects for the healthy growth of the international economy will be favorable. In that environment, with policy reforms effected in developing countries, prospects are good for their rapid growth and, with that, the creation of more markets for the developed countries as well as additional resources for environmental protection.

In such an environment, developing countries can achieve their objectives of rapid economic growth and rising living standards. They can move to become full partners in the strengthening of the global environment and economy. The rapid expansion of their markets, and their demands for imports, in turn, will provide significant benefits for the industrialized countries.

Comments

Benno J. Ndulu

My comments on Anne Krueger's book focus on four important issues concerning the costs and benefits to developing countries of participating in the ongoing process of the deeper integration of the world economy: the importance of integration into the world economy for developing countries; the conditions under which deeper integration can benefit the developing world; the prospects for the successful participation of the developing countries in the world economy given the third world's diverse conditions; and the appropriate mechanisms and time frame for fostering the deeper integration of the developing countries into the world economy.

Krueger recognizes that deeper integration offers both opportunities and constraints to growth and development and that accession to its agenda means weighing costs and benefits in the short and long term. The results and effectiveness of deeper integration in achieving growth and welfare affect the choices made by developing countries.

The Importance of Deeper Integration

That rapid growth of the international economy and world trade improves the growth prospects for the developing economies is be-

Benno Ndulu is executive director of the Africa Economic Research Consortium Program. He is currently on leave from the University of Dar es Salaam, where he is professor of economics.

coming widely accepted. Larger markets, access to better technology and learning through trade and international investment, and efficiency-enhancing competition offer developing economies opportunities for increased and diversified consumption as well as increased productivity. These opportunities assume a special importance for developing countries given their position as "late starters," presenting them with potential access to benefits from technological innovation (and investment) of the developed countries. Indeed the convergence of incomes, hypothesized and shown by endogenous growth literature, is to a large extent a result of this phenomenon, supporting the expectations of more rapid growth for developing countries who are in the process of catching up. World trade and international investment are the key instruments for realizing these opportunities.

Sebastian Edwards presents significant empirical evidence on the association between outer orientation and more rapid growth despite controversies about the extent of the connection.[1] These controversies relate to what constitutes trade liberalization and the relative importance of trade policy reforms in comparison with consistent macroeconomic policy in facilitating growth. Given the broad definition of outer orientation in this book, consistency of macroeconomic policy for a given trade regime is a crucial complement to trade policy.

Although cross-country studies by Barro and Lee, Easterly, and a few others have failed to find consistent evidence on the significant impact of openness to long-term growth, Edwards in a formal model, which assumes that a country's ability to absorb world technology depends on the openness of the economy and on a country's gap relative to the world in terms of total productivity, finds strong empirical evidence that open and less distorted trade regimes experienced higher total factor productivity growth.[2]

However, although international trade presents opportunities for faster growth to "late starters" via lower cost innovation, it also generates constraints because new industries may not be able to compete with those already established in developed countries, especially if a protective stance is adopted by the "early developers" as they seek deeper integration among themselves.

1. Edwards (1993).
2. Barro and Lee (1993); Easterly (1994); Edwards (1992).

The earlier concerns of Raúl Prebisch and H. W. Singer were that divergence in incomes and growing gaps between the developed and the developing world occurred because of secular declines in the prices of primary commodities. They made a case for structural diversification through industrialization to close the gap.[3] This aim remains a valid ambition for many developing countries especially in view of the more recent evidence by Reinhart and Wickham, which confirms the long-term decline of primary product prices in violent fluctuations since the 1970s.[4] What is important is the approach to industrialization that benefits from openness through export-led industrialization (rather than import substitution under protection). Whether the benefits accrue by way of higher marginal factor productivity and externalities from the export sector or through the role of export growth in alleviating the foreign exchange import constraint to growth, empirical results point to beneficial results of the open approach.[5]

However, a growing literature emphasizes the critical importance of human capacity, supportive infrastructure, and a mature institutional structure necessary for taking advantage of the opportunities for growth. "Conditional convergence" in long-term growth points to the fact that although "backwardness" usually fosters rapid growth, a country may be "too backward" and grow slowly.[6] On the one hand initial lower physical capital relative to human capital enhances total factor productivity and hence growth (the basis for unconditional income convergence), but on the other hand limited capacity to absorb or imitate technological progress may hamper rapid growth. Since many low-income countries are among those stagnating, evidently these countries have a very weak tendency, if any, toward unconditional convergence of incomes.[7]

Krueger's book does not adequately emphasize the importance of these complementary factors in exploiting opportunities offered by an efficient world economy. Literature now abounds to show that the phenomenal performance of Asian newly industrializing countries owes as much to these factors as to the outward orientation pursued by these countries.

3. Economic Commission for Latin America (1950); Singer (1950).
4. Reinhart and Wickham (1994).
5. See Feder (1983); Esfahami (1991); Helleiner (1986).
6. Easterly (1993).
7. Barro and Lee (1993).

Deeper Integration and Benefits to Developing Countries

The overriding concern of developing countries in the process of deeper integration of the world economy is increased market access for their goods. Previously they sought to achieve this access by arguing for preferential treatment in the world trading system. Now they are more often seeking access through mutual liberalization arrangements. The key questions are, what are the costs of this shift in approach, and what are the pay-offs? This is particularly important when one considers the additional requirements of deeper integration as a condition for improved market access. I agree with the thrust of the book that the process of deeper integration will prove beneficial to developing countries if two conditions are resultant: that market access expands and that the overall efficiency and size of the world economy increase.

The successful recent conclusion of the Uruguay Round saw a majority of developing countries signing on to the new approach to enlarging market access. To many of the countries this shift was helped along by their pursuit of unilateral liberalization and by the fact that only a handful of countries had significantly benefited from preferential treatment. However, for those countries that benefited, particularly southeast Asian countries, the shift represents a real scaling down of the double dividend enjoyed under the previous arrangement. It would be hard not to acknowledge that they profited immensely from the preferential treatment by setting themselves ahead of other developing countries. As the playing field is being leveled, part of that advantage is lost with the disappearance of preferential margins. One can only speculate about what the growth scenarios would have been like without the relative advantage that these countries made good use of.

The foregoing suggests to those countries that were not able to make good use of "free riding" that they tamper down their performance expectations as competition among developing countries intensifies for the limited market. This point makes the overall rapid growth of the world economy and its improved efficiency central to the realization of benefits under the new scenario.

The efficiency implications of premature enforcement of labor and environmental standards are also pertinent. To the extent that these measures stifle productivity growth and efficiency in developing countries they will prove detrimental to the prospects for development. Even more worrisome are the longer-term implications of an inability to utilize the comparative advantage these countries have in activities that make intensive use of unskilled labor. Krueger provides ample evidence from southeast Asia that countries who made use of their unskilled labor experienced not only an eventual shift in higher productivity growth but also, owing to higher growth in productivity, a convergence in wages with more developed countries.

For developing countries to make effective use of the new opportunities, therefore, access to international markets is fundamental. Trading arrangements that provide for deeper integration will be conducive to rapid growth of developing countries only if these arrangements do not hamper rapid growth of the international economy and world trade and do not constrain the realization of the comparative advantages of the developing countries, particularly unskilled labor activities. A shift of comparative advantages may be allowed to occur over time. As Krueger notes, the East Asian experience implies that a shift in comparative advantage is endogenous to the process of export-led growth and successful initial industrialization based on relatively abundant unskilled labor. Deeper integration schemes that penalize "outsiders" or transform nations into "fortresses" against less developed participants would be inimical to the growth of the international economy and world trade.

However, as Krueger argues, developing countries must adopt outer-oriented strategies and policies conducive to unconstrained interaction with the world economy to realize rapid growth. A domestic policy stance that limits access to international markets, international exchange, and investment limits the effective use of growth opportunities resulting from an expansion of world trade.

Prospects for Successful Deeper Integration

The prospects for developing countries to achieve deeper integration arise from the vast diversity among them in preconditions for doing so. These preconditions are characterized by openness to trade, competitiveness, and macroeconomic stability. However, domestic policy change toward outer orientation is not sufficient. Improved administrative capacity for compliance to the terms stipulated for deeper integration and political resources to sustain the major policy changes required are fundamental to a successful transition.

Deeper integration is a process of convergence in standards, conduct of policy, administrative capabilities, and institutional framework in an interdependent world. Krueger emphasizes policy convergence, especially openness to trade and competition policy, as the critical preconditions for deeper integration of the developing countries into the world economy. Domestic policy changes toward outer orientation are thus regarded as the necessary though not sufficient conditions for successful integration. Most of the developing countries are assessed to be still a long way off in meeting these conditions, and they have a limited administrative capacity to accede to most codes of deeper integration in the near future. Meeting preconditions for deeper integration presupposes attaining a phase of liberalization that entails a full liberalization of the current account and removal of all quantitative restrictions. I agree with the author that very few developing countries have reached this stage yet.

This view limits the scope for deeper integration to accession to schemes of the levels akin to those of the European Community and the North American Free Trade Agreement. The agenda for deeper integration is much broader in the global economy context, including different stages of policy harmonization and global interrelatedness. For countries furthest from the above description of liberalization, meeting the "preconditions" for deeper integration identified in this book is part of the integration process. In line with this broader view, an acceleration of deeper integration has occurred, judging from the recent pace of reforms in developing countries and the rapidly growing share of world trade in output.[8]

The willingness of many of these countries to sign on to the Uruguay Round accord has been facilitated by this recent development. Four main reasons are responsible for this acceleration, and three of them can be attributed to external pressure:[9]

—Multilateral trade arrangements under GATT have increasingly attached conditionality for most favored nations status and graduation clauses under differential treatment to prevent abuse of article XVIII.

8. Tanzi (1995).
9. Haggard (1995).

—High conditionality imposed for structural adjustment lending and aid has gone beyond macroeconomic stabilization and a relative shift toward production of tradables to encompass supply-side measures including trade policy reforms (including international taxation), dismantling of quantitative restrictions, and liberalization of payment arrangements; industrial policy, financial liberalization, privatization (including the adoption of more open foreign investment codes), and improved governance. International financial institutions, supplemented by bilateral aid programs, have been the key enforcers of high conditionality.

—Bilateral reciprocity—directed at market opening to counter the so-called unfair trade practices and bilateral investment treaties. This mechanism emphasizes reciprocated threat (but if occurring among unequals is effectively a one-way threat).

—Domestic pressures for liberalization have grown in reaction to control regimes of the past that taxed exporters; the light-bulb effects of success stories; political change; and shifting business interests toward partnership with outsiders.

By far, the external pressures have been the most significant in initiating changes, prompting some doubts on their sustainability in the event of reduction of high-conditionality lending. A lot depends on the internalization of the reform process and the strength of the new local constituency for reforms. The effectiveness of these reforms in achieving results will foster credibility and sustain the changes. Protective reactions by developed countries to successful performance will only undermine the process of change as such reactions will reduce the yield from reforms.

Deeper integration is a process involving different stages of achievement. With that thought in mind, in my opinion prospects for successful integration of the developing countries into the world economy are more optimistic than what is reflected in this book.

Mechanisms for Fostering Deeper Integration

What mechanisms and arrangements would foster an accelerated deeper integration into the world economy of developing economies that are at different stages of development and have varying capacities to accede to the deeper integration agenda?

Three considerations are important. The first is the need to accommodate diversity in the initial conditions without engendering complacence. Fairness in the treatment of unequals should be emphasized. Second, the time frame for convergence must take into account differential adjustment costs for each category of developing countries. Convergence entails different levels of adjustments and costs. In weighing costs and benefits to accession for different groups of countries, the optimal pace and scope of adjustment must be determined. Third, the adjustment process, particularly for those least developed countries, must be financed to partially alleviate adjustment costs for accelerated integration. More important, technical and financial support is needed to address limitations of administrative capacity to accede to the agenda of deeper integration. Support for putting in place a legal framework that makes contracts enforceable, protection of property rights, and reduction in transactions costs associated with nontransparent institutional structures are fundamental. These needs must be met in addition to aiding the establishment of transparent and efficient markets and building human capacity and infrastructure.

Hence the arrangements to foster deeper integration must provide for the following:

—Differential treatment based on differences in initial conditions. Flexible but graduated standards should allow a time-bound phasing for meeting clearly established conditions (a point made in the book). GATT conditions under the recently concluded Uruguay Round already provide flexibility but need further explication of benchmarks for the different categories of developing countries.

—Accommodation of different speeds of adjustment. Political resources and shock treatment versus gradualism must be considered.

—Access to markets at least at the current GATT terms (again a point made in the book).

—A combination of global pressure and domestic initiative in sustaining the process of reform. Global pressure should complement the more important domestic ownership of such reforms. Transparent rule-based multilateral pressure rather than discretionary arrangements under bilateralism is preferable.

—Conviction from tangible results rather than coercion. Successful results provide a strong basis for sustainable reforms.

Dani Rodrik

Anne Krueger has written a sensible book that packs a lot of wisdom into a relatively small space. It is difficult to disagree with many of her broad themes—such as the importance of the health of the global economy to the performance of developing countries (LDCs), the diversity of starting points among LDCs, or the preferability of bringing LDCs into deep integration via carrots rather than sticks. The last point, in particular, is of great importance but may well fall on deaf ears. Rather than repeat the conclusions with which I agree, I will use this space to raise some issues that require more elaboration or on which our perspectives differ somewhat.

The Relationship between Trade Strategy and Economic Growth

Krueger spends the better part of a chapter reviewing the experiences of developing countries with trade. This is important insofar as it helps us gauge the stakes that developing countries have in the health of the international trading system. The bottom line, worth repeating, is that the countries that have been the most successful are also the ones that have taken the most advantage of trade opportunities. East Asian countries, in particular, have experienced unprecedented rates of growth since the 1960s in the context of rapidly expanding exports (and imports). Those countries that have rigidly followed import-substitution policies and erected barriers against exports have lagged behind. Trade has been a friend of economic development and growth, not an enemy, as many policymakers and economists had feared in the immediate postwar period.

That much is clear. What is far less clear is the extent to which trade and trade policies have played a causal role in economic growth. Krueger's views on this subject are well known. Indeed, she presents East Asia's economic performance as one of "export-led growth," a characterization that, thanks in no small part to Krueger's own earlier work, has become part and parcel of the conventional wisdom on East Asia.

Dani Rodrik is professor of economics and international affairs at Columbia University.

The story that Krueger lays out goes as follows. Following a relatively short bout with import-substitution policies in the 1950s, South Korea and Taiwan shifted to more neutral, and relatively uniform, incentives, eliminating the earlier bias against exports. This switch led to specialization in line with these countries' comparative advantage in labor-intensive manufactures. As trade expanded, so did economic activity, and the eventual sophistication of the kind of goods produced and sold on world markets.

But consider an alternative scenario, which has as its starting point another aspect of Korea's and Taiwan's reforms around 1960: the concerted attempt by both governments to increase private investment. Let us follow through the implications, on the assumption that the investment incentives were successful in eliciting private investment. (Indeed, a sharp rise in investment took place in both countries in the early 1960s.) Since neither country had much of a capital-goods industry, increased investment required increased imports. External borrowing opportunities being limited, that in turn required a rise in exports to pay for the imports. In this scenario, a rising export-GDP ratio would be a consequence of the increase in investment demand (and not its instigator). Exports would be important as a facilitator of growth, but they would not be its determinant.

Why ruin a perfectly acceptable story by considering such an alternative possibility? For the simple reason that the conventional story does not quite fit the facts. For example, it is quite plausible that, as Krueger discusses, the measured antiexport bias in Korea in the 1960s was small, and possibly nonexistent. However, the calculations that show this result also reveal a puzzling finding when carried back to the 1950s: the bias in favor of exports turns out to have been significantly greater in the second half of the 1950s![1] In other words, there is no indication of a sizable change in incentives toward exportables in the early 1960s when exports started to boom. The same is true of Taiwan, where most of the pro-export incentives were put in place in the late 1950s.[2] The export-led story is problematic for an even simpler reason as well. As Krueger notes, in both countries exports were a small share of national income early on. In South Korea, exports were less than 5 percent of GNP in 1960, and manu-

1. Frank, Kim, and Westphal (1975).
2. See Rodrik (forthcoming) for more details.

factured exports were only a tiny fraction of that. No matter what the posited linkage between exports and growth, that such a small base could have propelled the economy forward in a quantitatively significant way is implausible.

The point is not to denigrate the role of trade and its importance for economic development. The cross-country evidence is fairly convincing on the importance of trade. Rather, the point is to suggest that developing countries are likely to be disappointed if they come to rely on open trade policies as their main growth-promoting strategy. The real lesson that should be drawn from the East Asian experience is the importance of having an investment strategy along with a trade strategy.

The Role of Investment

It has become fashionable in development policy circles to downplay the importance of investment for economic growth. This view is partly a reaction to early postwar thinking, which viewed capital accumulation as the central problem of development and neglected the role of prices and of allocative efficiency. Krueger emphasizes at several junctures that the importance of investment was oversold to developing country policymakers and that many countries that managed to increase their investment rates did not experience high growth.

Ironically, this downplaying of investment comes when a broad range of empirical studies of growth have uncovered that investment, after all, is central to growth. Cross-country regression analyses have found that physical investment is one of the strongest determinants of growth. Furthermore, it is practically the only variable that is robustly correlated with growth in the sense that its statistical significance is unaffected by the inclusion of a broad range of additional variables on the right-hand side of the regression.[3] Of course, this does not preclude the existence of some countries with low growth despite high investment. But such cases are the exception rather than the rule.

Careful analysis of the East Asian growth miracles has revealed that high growth is largely attributable to accumulation (in physical and

3. Levine and Renelt (1992).

human capital) rather than total factor productivity (TFP) growth[4]
The implication, once again, is that investment is central to growth.
The secrets of success lie in the ability to lift investment by raising the
private returns to accumulation.

The Drawbacks of Import-Substitution Strategies

On balance, import-substitution policies engendered large inefficiencies by divorcing production and investment decisions from
world prices. Krueger's account amply documents these costs. However, as Krueger notes, some of the leading import-substituting countries like Brazil and Turkey had respectable growth rates (around 6
percent a year) over long stretches. What ultimately did such countries in was the periodic balance-of-payments crises to which their
economies succumbed. So the most damning comment one can make
about import-substitution policies is that they were also responsible
for these periodic crises. Krueger clearly believes that they were:
"vulnerability from the consequences of import substitution . . . led to
foreign exchange crises." (chap. 1).

This charge against import-substitution policies would probably
not stand up in court. Essentially, the argument neglects the fact that
any degree of trade protection is compatible with macroeconomic
stability and external balance. There is nothing inherently prone to
instability or stop-go policies in import substitution. Indeed, many
import-substituting countries have managed to avoid protracted external crises thanks to sound fiscal and exchange-rate policies. India
is an example: Indian policymakers managed to avoid serious balance-of-payments problems until 1991, and the crisis of 1991 was
promptly dealt with. On the other hand, export-oriented countries
have also been prone to payments crises when their macroeconomic
policies have gone astray. Korea had a severe macrocrisis in 1979–80,
following a bout of overspending. The Turkish economy, which made
its transition to outer-oriented policies in 1980, crashed in 1994 as a
result of sustained fiscal laxity. Mexico, which turned outward in the
mid-1980s, experienced a sudden withdrawal of funds in late 1994 as
a result of nervousness about an overvalued exchange rate and elec-

4. Kim and Lau (1992); Young (1994).

tion-time credit expansion. A payments crisis is the fate that awaits any government that ignores budget constraints, regardless of its trade strategy.

Implications of the Uruguay Round for the Developing Countries

Krueger judges the Uruguay Round to be largely a success for developing countries. She counts the agreements on agriculture and the Multifiber Arrangement as a net gain, with the TRIPs agreement posing only short-term costs to the lower-income countries. Most of the other "concessions" (such as the increased tariff bindings and the TRIMs agreement) are, according to Krueger, good policy to begin with.

I am somewhat less bullish on the Uruguay Round. First, the agreement on agriculture does raise the possibility that food-importing developing countries will suffer terms-of-trade losses. Second, the backloading of the liberalization of the Multifiber Arrangement raises serious concerns about the dynamic consistency of the commitment made by the importing countries. Can one really believe that the governments of these countries will comply with a rule that requires half of all quotas existing today to be eliminated overnight when the deadline arrives ten years from now?

However, the most important source of gain for developing countries may well be the new dispute settlement mechanism of the World Trade Organization, something that Krueger does not discuss. Under the former set of rules, any country, including the target of a complaint, could block a GATT panel ruling. Now, blocking a panel ruling requires a unanimous vote. (There is an added appellate procedure, however.) Developing countries have traditionally made very little use of the GATT's dispute settlement procedure. And for good reason, given the weakness of the procedures. If the new rules prove as promising as they sound, developing countries, which are usually the weak side in any bargaining situation, could well end up as the primary beneficiary.

Deep Integration

Despite occasional caveats, the hypothesis maintained in the book is that we can treat deep integration (or, more to the point, developing countries can treat deep integration) as pretty much the same as an intensification of free trade in goods and services. In other words, deep integration is just like free trade; only, it goes a little bit "deeper." A corollary, also evident as a maintained hypothesis, is that deep integration is a continuation of, or a natural follow-up on, the policy reforms undertaken recently by many countries in Latin America (and before them in East Asia). Krueger does not explicitly say these things, but I think I am giving an accurate characterization of her views.

The problem is that deep integration is not simply "more of the same." It is quite a different animal. The Brookings project description defines deep integration, appropriately I think, as "the harmonization and possibly coordination of economic policies and domestic laws and institutions." Now, ask yourself how much economists know about the desirability of "harmonization in domestic laws and institutions." And compare the answer to how much economists know about the desirability of free trade in goods, services, and capital (that is, shallow integration). The answer to the second question should be "a lot"; the intellectually honest answer to the first question, however, would be that economists do not even know how to think about that question.

A direct analogy with shallow integration may be helpful. It may be tempting to think of deep integration as a form of free trade in institutions and to presume that international arbitrage in laws, regulations, and institutions can improve welfare in the same manner that arbitrage in commodities does. But even stating the issue in such terms reveals how absurd the analogy is. What's involved in deep integration is not the enabling of consumers, citizens, or nations to choose their own institutions; quite the contrary, what's involved is the imposition of restrictions to doing so. Harmonization implies the imposition of a uniform set of institutions. What's worse is that the institutions that are likely to serves as focal points around which harmonization occurs are likely to be determined by politics, that is, by power.

Why does this matter? It matters because a recognition that shallow and deep integration are qualitatively different guards against excessive and misplaced enthusiasm about the consequences of deep integration for LDCs. It also matters because it underscores that the implications of deep integration are more complex and less predictable than simple extrapolations from shallow integration would indicate. Consequently, the specifics of the various issues must be closely examined.

More concretely, I would argue that deep integration carries a substantial downside risk for LDCs, as well as a substantial upside potential. On the downside, consider the three areas that are probably of highest concern to developing countries: labor standards, environmental protection, and intellectual property rights. In each one, deep integration poses significant risks to the interests of developing countries.

The threats of labor standards are obvious, and Krueger appropriately discusses them at length. Although regulations against, say, the use of prison labor or child labor may not be hard to justify on moral and humanitarian grounds, there can be little doubt that many other standards that arise in this context are motivated by protectionist impulses in developed countries. Even with a relatively clean issue such as the use of child labor, it is far from clear that internationally negotiated standards can improve the well-being of the intended beneficiaries—in this case, children.

Similarly, environmental concerns too often hide protectionist motives as well. This reality was all too evident during the debate on the North American Free Trade Agreement (NAFTA). Surely, there may be legitimate international concerns about environmental degradation in poor countries. But equally surely, these concerns ought not be linked with trade issues, and they should be raised and dealt with in appropriate forums.

Finally, intellectual property rights, or TRIPs. Despite much obfuscation on this issue, most developing countries stand to gain very little and a few could lose quite a bit by tightening protection of foreigners' intellectual property rights. As a coauthor of one of the few theoretical papers trying to make the case in favor of TRIPs from the LDC perspective, I can vouch for the difficulty of building a logically coherent argument in this direction.[5] Since developing country policies are unlikely to have much of an impact on global innovative activity, tighter patent or copyright protection entails, in the first instance, a redistribution of income from poor to rich countries. Efficiency consequences tend to be of second-order importance compared with this redistributive outcome.

5. Diwan and Rodrik (1991).

Remember that most of the successful East Asian economies that Krueger cites approvingly have prospered in environments with no externally imposed constraints on labor, the environment, or standards on intellectual property. The institutional choices made by these successful economies bear scant resemblance to what is observed in OECD countries. The United States has long sought to impose tighter restrictions on patents and copyrights in countries like Korea and Taiwan. In labor markets, Korean or Singaporean labor practices have differed substantially from OECD ones. In the area of competition policy, the Japanese or Korean approach, with its emphasis on avoiding "excess competition," diverges fundamentally from the Western one. Some would argue that these institutional distinctions have been critical to the exemplary growth performance of the East Asian countries. At the very least, clearly these countries were not harmed by having made a different set of legal or institutional choices. Hence, in all of these areas (labor, environment, TRIPs, competition policy), the LDCs have little to be enthusiastic about and much to worry about.

The integration experience of the Mediterranean countries in the European Union makes a useful case study. Krueger's discussion, however, downplays too much one very important advantage that Spain, Portugal, and Greece have had: huge capital inflows from abroad, both official and private, associated with their membership in the European Union. Under the EU's structural funds alone, Greece and Portugal receive between $1 billion and $2 billion annually (which amounts to $100 to $200 a person), and Spain receives close to $3 billion a year.[6] Both Spain and Portugal (but not Greece) have experienced an explosion in inward direct foreign investment (see figures 1, 2, and 3). Neither of these sources of capital is likely to be available to other LDCs venturing into deep integration: official sources will be lacking for obvious reasons, and direct foreign investment will not flow as easily into countries that do not possess the geographical advantage that the Mediterranean countries (or Mexico in the context of NAFTA) have. So one must be careful in extrapolating from the EU experience to other LDCs.

---

6. Many different funds cover several different objectives: objective 1 (regional development); 2 (decline of traditional industries); 3 (long-term unemployment); 4 (assistance for young people to get jobs); 5a (modernization of farms); 5b (rural areas).

Figure 1. *Official Transfers and DFI Inflows in Greece*

Percent of GNP

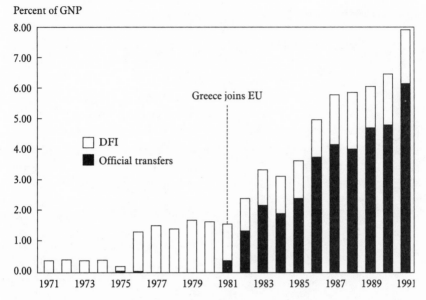

Source: author's calculations based on data from IMF, *International Financial Statistics*, various issues.

Figure 2. *Official Transfers and DFI Inflows in Portugal*

Percent of GNP

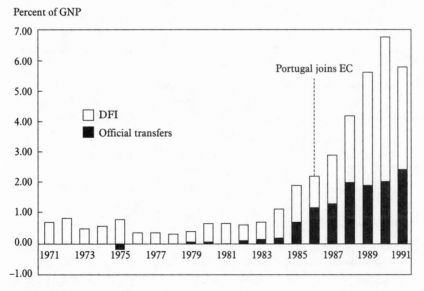

Source: See figure 1.

Figure 3. *Official Transfers and DFI Inflows in Spain*

Percent of GNP

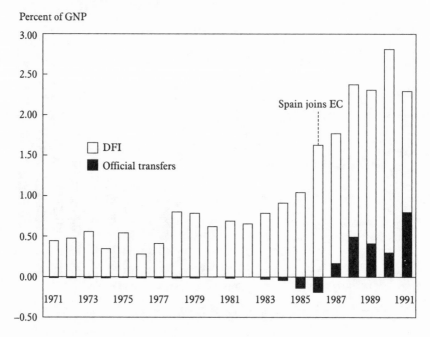

Source: See figure 1.

But as I mentioned earlier, there is also an upside for LDCs. The "harmonization in domestic laws and institutions" entailed by deep integration presents an opportunity for reformist governments in developing countries to "lock in" their reforms and render them irreversible. It is no secret that Carlos Salinas wanted NAFTA at least as badly for its potential role in cementing Mexico's institutional reforms since 1986 as for its market-access provisions. Arguably, the EU's greatest contribution to the long-run prosperity and stability of Spain, Portugal, and Greece resides in its having made a return to military rule in these countries virtually impossible.

To appreciate the full potential of deep integration along this dimension, consider the following thought experiment: suppose that Bolivia or Ghana could overnight harmonize their trade and industrial policymaking machinery with that of the EU. By this I mean that Bolivia and Ghana would not only adopt the same regulations as those prevailing in the EU, but they would also commit to refraining from changing these regulations without the EU's consent. What would be the outcome? My guess is that economic performance in these two countries would improve considerably. Not because EU policies are inherently more desirable. Certainly not: Bolivia for one has a much cleaner trade regime than does the EU. But because harmonization would probably result in an enhancement of the private sector's expectations about the stability and predictability of the policy regime, as well as an enhancement of the respect for private enterprise, property, enforcement of contracts, and the rule of law. Or, to look at the same question from the opposite end, consider Puerto Rico, and whether Puerto Rico would not look more like Haiti or the Dominican Republic if it did not operate under the framework of U.S. laws and institutions.

In other words, what deep integration could contribute to countries like Bolivia and Ghana, where uncertainty, unpredictability, and rent-seeking have been rife, is an improvement not in policy but in policymaking. And that in itself could have tremendous payoff.

Now I will admit immediately that this argument is purely speculative. Moreover, some may find the whole idea too reminiscent of colonialism for comfort. But I do think that the notion of deep integration as a "commitment technology" is valid for reformist governments who want to signal to their private sectors that the rules of the game are now changing for good.

Thinking about deep integration in this fashion may well change some of the conclusions offered by Krueger. For example, Krueger argues that countries that have not yet undertaken shallow-integration reforms must do so before they contemplate deep integration and that a transition period may be required for phasing the latter in. But once deep integration is viewed as a commitment technology that allows the governments in developing countries to buy into more credible Northern institutions, this sequencing makes much less sense. The countries that need deep integration the most may well be the ones that have managed to reform the least.

To summarize, deep integration is at once a threat and an opportunity for developing countries. The challenge to the world community at large is to minimize the threat while maximizing the opportunity. The task for analysts is to show how this can be done. That, I think, requires a more in-depth—and a more speculative—analysis of the specific issues contained in the deep integration agenda, as well as of the institutional bases and consequences of deep integration.

References

Anderson, Kym, ed. 1992. *New Silk Roads: East Asia and World Textile Markets.* New York: Cambridge University Press.

Baldwin, Robert E. 1994. "An Economic Evaluation of the Uruguay Round Agreements." Paper presented at "Beyond the Uruguay Round: Environment, Competition and Regulation." NBER conference, Washington, October 28.

Baldwin, Robert E., and Tracy Murray. 1977. "MFN Tariff Reductions and Developing Country Trade Benefits under the GSP." *Economic Journal* 87 (March): 30–46.

Baldwin, Robert E. 1969. "The Case against Infant-Industry Tariff Protection." *Journal of Political Economy* 77 (May-June): 295–305.

Barro, R. J. and Wash Lee. 1993. "Losers and Winners in Economic Growth." In *Proceedings of the World Bank Annual Conference on Development Economics,* edited by Laurence H. Summers and Shekhar Shah. Washington: World Bank.

Bates, Robert H., and Anne O. Krueger, eds. 1993. *Political and Economic Interactions in Economic Policy Reform: Evidence from Eight Countries.* Cambridge, Mass.: Basil Blackwell.

Bhagwati, Jagdish N. 1978. *Foreign Trade Regimes and Economic Development: Vol. 11: Anatomy and Consequences of Exchange Control Regimes.* Columbia University Press for the National Bureau of Economic Research.

Bhagwati, Jagdish N., and T. N. Srinivasan. 1974. "On Reanalyzing the Harris-Todaro Model: Policy Rankings in the Case of Sector-Specific Sticky Wages." *American Economic Review* 64 (June): 502–8.

———. 1975. *Foreign Trade Regimes and Economic Development: Vol. 6: India.* Columbia University Press for the National Bureau of Economic Research.

Chenery, Hollis B., and Alan M. Strout. 1966. "Foreign Assistance and Economic Development." *American Economic Review* 56 (September): 679–733.

Chin, Judith, and Gene Grossman. 1990. "Intellectual Property Rights and North-South Trade." In *Political Economy of International Trade,* edited by Ronald W. Jones and Anne O. Krueger, 90–107. Cambridge, Mass.: Basil Blackwell.

Cline, William R., and Sidney Weintraub, eds. 1981. *Economic Stabilization in Developing Countries.* Brookings.

Cooper, Richard N. 1994. *Environment and Resource Policies for the World Economy.* Brookings.

Corbo, Vittorio, and Jaime de Melo. 1987. "Lessons from the Southern Cone Policy Reforms." *World Bank Research Observer* 2 (July): lll-42.

Dam, Kenneth W. 1970. *The GATT: Law and the International Economic Organization.* University of Chicago Press.

Deardorff, Alan V. 1992. "Welfare Effects of Global Patent Protection." *Economica* 59 (February): 35–51.

———. 1994. "Economic Effects of Tariff and Quota Reductions." In *The New GATT: Implications for the United States,* edited by Susan M. Collins and Barry P. Bosworth, 7–27. Brookings.

Diaz-Alejandro, Carlos F. 1965. "On the Import-Intensity of Import Substitution." *Kyklos* 18 (3): 495–511.

Diwan, Ishak, and Dani Rodrik. 1991. "Patents, Appropriate Technology, and North-South Trade." *Journal of International Economics* 30 (February): 27–48.

Donges, Juergen B., and Klaus-Werner Schatz. 1989. "The Iberian Countries in the EEC: Risks and Changes for their Manufacturing Industries." In *European Integration and the Iberian Economies,* edited by George N. Yannapoulos. Basingstoke: Macmillan.

Easterly, William. 1993. "How Much Do Distortions Affect Growth?" *Journal of Monetary Economics* 32 (November): 187–212.

———. 1994. "Economic Stagnation, Fixed Factors, and Policy Thresholds." *Journal of Monetary Economics* 33 (June): 525–57.

Economic Commission for Latin America. 1950. *The Economic Development of Latin America and Its Principal Problems.* New York: United Nations.

Edwards, Sebastian. 1993. "Openness, Trade Liberalization and Growth in Developing Countries." *Journal of Economic Literature* 31 (September): 1358–93.

———. 1992. "Trade Orientation, Distortions and Growth in Developing Countries." *Journal of Development Economics* 39 (July): 31–57.

Ehrenberg, Ronald G. 1994. *Labor Markets and Integrating National Economies.* Brookings.

Esfahani, Hadi S. 1991. "Exports, Imports, and Economic Growth in Semi-Industrialized Countries" *Journal of Development Economics* 35 (January): 93–116.

Evenson, Robert. 1978. "The Organization of Research to Improve Crops and Animals in Low-Income Countries." In *Distortions of Agricultural Incentives,* edited by Theodore W. Schultz, 223–45. University of Indiana Press.

Feder, Gershon. 1983. "On Exports and Economic Growth." *Journal of Development Economics* 12 (February-April): 59–73.

Fields, Gary S. 1989. "On the Job Search in a Labor Market Model: Ex Ante Choices and Ex Post Outcomes." *Journal of Development Economics* 30 (January): 159–78.

Fields, Gary S. 1994. "Changing Labor Market Conditions and Economic Development in Hong Kong, the Republic of Korea, Singapore, and Taiwan, China." *World Bank Economic Review* 8 (September): 395–414.

Frank, Charles R. Jr., Kwang Suk Kim, and Larry E. Westphal. 1975. *Foreign Trade Regimes and Economic Development: Vol. 7: South Korea*. Columbia University Press for the National Bureau of Economic Research.

Frank, Isaiah. 1979. "The Graduation Issue for LDC's." *Journal of World Trade Law* 13 (July-August): 289–302.

General Agreement on Tariffs and Trade. 1992. *International Trade 1990–91*. Geneva.

Gregory, Peter, and Lloyd Reynolds. 1965. *Wages, Productivity and Industrialization in Puerto Rico*. Homewood, Ill.: Richard D. Irwin.

Grilli, Enzo. 1990. "Responses of Developing Countries to Trade Protectionism in Developed Countries." In *The Direction of Trade Policy*, edited by Charles S. Pearson and James Riedel, 108–29. Cambridge, Mass.: Basil Blackwell.

Grossman, Gene M., and Alan B. Krueger. 1991. "Environmental Impacts of a North American Free Trade Agreement." Working Paper 3914. Cambridge, Mass.: National Bureau of Economic Research (November).

Haggard, Stephan. 1995. *Developing Nations and the Politics of Global Integration*. Brookings.

Harris, John R., and Michael P. Todaro. 1970. "Migration, Unemployment and Development: A Two-Sector Analysis." *American Economic Review* 60 (March): 126–42.

Helleiner, Gerald K. 1986. "Outward Orientation, Import Instability and African Economic Growth: An Empirical Investigation." In *Theory and Reality in Development*, edited by Sanjaya Lall and Frances Stewart. St. Martin's Press.

Hindley, Brian. 1987. "Different and More Favorable Treatment—and Graduation." In *The Uruguay Round. A Handbook on the Multilateral Trade Negotiations*, edited by J. Michael Finger and Andrzej Olechowski, 67–74. Washington: World Bank.

Hine, James. 1989. "Customs Union Enlargement and Adjustment: Spain's Accession to the European Community." *Journal of Common Market Studies* 28 (September): 1-27.

Hoekman, Bernard. 1994. "Services and Intellectual Property Rights." In *The New GATT: Implications for the United States*, edited by Susan M. Collins and Barry P. Bosworth, 84–110. Brookings.

Hong, Wontack, 1981. "Export Promotion and Employment Growth in South Korea." In *Trade and Employment in Developing Countries: Vol. 1: Individual Studies*, edited by Anne O. Krueger and others, 341–92. University of Chicago Press for the National Bureau of Economic Research.

Hufbauer, Gary Clyde, and Kimberley Ann Elliot. 1994. *Measuring the Costs of Protection in the United States*. Washington: Institute for International Economics.

Hufbauer, Gary Clyde., and Jeffrey J. Schott. 1992. *North American Free Trade: Issues and Recommendations*. Washington: Institute for International Economics.

International Labor Organization. 1993. *Yearbook of Labor Statistics*. Geneva.

———. 1994. *Yearbook of Labor Statistics*. Geneva.

International Monetary Fund. 1983. *International Financial Statistics*. Washington.

———. 1993. *International Financial Statistics*. August, Washington.

———. 1993. *International Financial Statistics Yearbook*. Washington.

Johnson, Harry G. 1967. *Economic Policies toward Less Developed Countries.* Brookings.

Karsenty, Guy, and Sam Laird. 1987. "The GSP, Policy Options and the New Round." *Weltwirtschaftliches Archiv.* 123 (2): 262–96.

Keesing, Donald B., and Martin Wolf. 1980. *Textile Quotas against Developing Countries.* London: Trade Policy Research Centre.

Kim, J.I., and L.J. Lau. 1992. "The Sources of Economic Growth of the Newly Industrialized Countries on the Pacific Rim." Stanford University (December).

Kim, Kwang Suk, and Michael Roemer. 1979. *Growth and Structural Transformation: Studies in the Modernization of the Republic of Korea, 1945–1975.* Harvard University Press.

Krueger, Anne O. 1975. *Foreign Trade Regimes and Economic Development: Vol. 1: Turkey.* Columbia University Press for the National Bureau of Economic Research.

———. 1979. *The Developmental Role of the Foreign Sector and Aid.* Harvard University Press.

Krueger, Anne O., and others, eds. 1981. *Trade and Employment in Developing Countries: Vol. l: Individual Studies.* University of Chicago Press for the National Bureau of Economic Research.

Krueger, Anne O., ed. 1983. *Trade and Employment in Developing Countries: Synthesis and Conclusions.* University of Chicago Press.

Krueger, Anne O. 1984. "Comparative Advantage and Development Policy 20 Years Later." In *Economic Structure and Performance,* edited by Moshe Syrquin, Lance Taylor, and Larry E. Westphal, 135–56. Orlando: Academic Press.

———. 1987. "Importance of Economic Policy in Develoment: Contrasts between Korea and Turkey." In *Protection and Competition in International Trade,* edited by Henry Kierzkowski, 172–203. Cambridge, Mass.: Basil Blackwell.

Krueger, Anne O., and others. 1989. *Aid and Development.* Johns Hopkins University Press.

Krueger, Anne O. 1990a. "Economists' Changing Perceptions of Government." *Weltwirtschaftliches Archiv* 126 (3) 417–31.

———. 1990b. "Trends in Trade Policies of Developing Countries." In *The Direction of Trade Policy,* edited by Charles S. Pearson and James Riedel, 87–107. Cambridge, Mass.: Basil Blackwell.

Krueger, Anne O., and Okan H. Aktan. 1992. *Swimming against the Tide: Turkish Trade Reform in the 1980s.* San Francisco: ICS Press.

Krueger, Anne O., and Ilter Turan. 1993. "The Politics and Economics of Turkish Policy Reforms in the 1980s." In *Political and Economic Interactions in Economic Policy Reform,* edited by Robert H. Bates and Anne O. Krueger, 333–86. Cambridge, Mass.: Basil Blackwell.

Kuo, Shirley W.Y. 1983. *The Taiwan Economy in Transition.* Westview Press.

Levine, Ross, and David Renelt. 1992. "A Sensitivity Analysis of Cross-Country Growth Regressions." *American Economic Review* 82 (September): 942–63.

Marks, Stephen V., and Keith E. Maskus. 1993. *The Economics and Politics of World Sugar Policies.* University of Michigan Press.

Mason, Edward S., and others. 1980. *The Economic and Social Modernization of the Republic of Korea.* Harvard University Press.

Morawetz, David. 1978. *Twenty-Five Years of Economic Development 1950-1975.* Johns Hopkins University Press.

Organization for Economic Cooperation and Development. 1991. *OECD Economic Surveys: Spain.*

Reinhart, Carmen M., and Peter Wickham. 1994. "Commodity Prices: Cyclical Weakness or Secular Decline?" International Monetary Fund Working Paper 94/7. Washington (January).

Rodrik, Dani. 1993. "Trade and Industrial Policy Reform in Developing Countries: A Review of Recent Theory and Evidence." Working Paper 4417. Cambridge, Mass: National Bureau of Economic Research (August).

———. 1994. "Developing Countries after the Uruguay Round." Paper prepared for the Group of Twenty-Four, New York (August).

———. Forthcoming. "Getting Interventions Right: How South Korea and Taiwan Grew Rich." *Economic Policy.*

Sachs, Jeffrey D. 1985. "External Debt and Macreconomic Performance in Latin America and East Asia." *Brookings Papers on Economic Activity* 2: 523–73.

Schiff, Maurice, and Alberto Valdes. 1990. *Political Economy of Agricultural Pricing Policies in Developing Countries,* vol. 4. Johns Hopkins University Press.

Shirk, Susan L. 1994. *How China Opened Its Door: The Political Success of the PRC's Foreign Trade and Investment Reforms.* Brookings.

Singer, H. W. 1950. "The Distribution of Gains between Investing and Borrowing Countries." *American Economic Review* 40 (May): 473–85.

Sturc, Ernest. 1968. "Stabilization Policies: Experience of Some European Countries in the 1950s." *International Monetary Fund Staff Papers* 15 (July): 197–219.

Tanzi, Vito. 1995. *Taxation in an Integrating World.* Brookings.

United Nations. 1990. *Handbook of International Trade and Development Statistics 1989.* New York.

Williamson, John, ed. 1983. *IMF Conditionality.* Washington: Institute for International Economics.

Wolf, Martin. 1987. "Differential and More Favorable Treatment of Developing Countries and the International Trading System." *World Bank Economic Review* 1 (September): 647–68.

World Bank. 1982. *World Development Report.* Oxford University Press.

———. 1983. *World Development Report.* Oxford University Press.

———. 1985. *World Development Report.* Oxford University Press.

———. 1986. *World Development Report.* Oxford University Press.

———. 1991. *World Development Report.* Oxford University Press.

———. 1993a. *World Development Report.* Oxford University Press.

———. 1993b. *The East Asian Miracle: Economic Growth and Public Policy.* Oxford University Press.

Young, A. 1994. "The Tyranny of Numbers: Confronting the Statistical Realities of the East Asian Growth Experience." Massachusetts Institute of Technology (February).

Zietz, Joachim, and Alberto Valdés. 1993. "The Growth of Agricultural Production." In *Trade and Protectionism,* edited by Takatoshi Ito and Anne O. Krueger, 115–49. University of Chicago Press.

Index